HOW TO WRITE
AND SPEAK
IN BUSINESS

HOW TO WRITE
AND SPEAK
IN BUSINESS

Richard A. Kaumeyer, Jr.

VNR VAN NOSTRAND REINHOLD COMPANY
—————— New York ——————

Library of Congress Catalog Card Number: 84-10466
ISBN: 0-442-21333-6

Manufactured in the United States of America

Published by Van Nostrand Reinhold Company Inc.
135 West 50th Street
New York, New York 10020

Van Nostrand Reinhold Company Limited
Molly Millars Lane
Wokingham, Berkshire RG11 2PY, England

Van Nostrand Reinhold
480 Latrobe Street
Melbourne, Victoria 3000, Australia

Macmillan of Canada
Division of Gage Publishing Limited
164 Commander Boulevard
Agincourt, Ontario M1S 3C7, Canada

Library of Congress Cataloging in Publication Data

Kaumeyer, Jr., Richard A.
  How to write and speak in business.
  Includes index.

  1. Communication in management.   I. Title.
HF5718.K38   1984   658.4'5   84-10466
ISBN 0-442-21333-6

To my parents:
Richard A., Sr. and Lauretta Edna Kaumeyer

Preface

This book is based on the author's notes from a series of seminars conducted over the years on the topic of business communications. These seminars were given to business audiences—people who were looking for results. The feedback after the seminars indicated the information was useful. It was something the participants took back and applied to communications problems in the workplace.

The aim has been to provide the reader with some basic steps to improve his or her skills in business writing or giving a business presentation. The material has been "field tested" so to speak by businessmen and women who tried it and came back to comment favorably on the results. The emphasis is on the practical rather than the theoretical approach.

There are numerous examples and illustrations provided to supplement the reading. They are deliberately not technical in nature, but are based on the old adage that "a picture is worth a thousand words."

Most of the tips, hints, tricks, and so on are not new or unique. They are basic and the professionals will say—"Hey, I know that and do it all the time." But most people in business do not consider themselves professional memo writers or business speakers. It is at this audience that the book is aimed. It is often the simple techniques that make or break someone in the business world. There is an old saying that if you come away from a seminar with one idea or concept that you weren't familiar with it was worth the time. A poll of those in the seminars on which this book is based indicated that the audience usually came away with eight to twelve items. Not that the ideas discussed were new or unique, but that they hadn't been developed in exactly that way before.

Because of work pressures, those in business are often limited in the exposure they get to new ideas. Their experiences are limited to the people they come in contact with as part of their specific environment. There is only a limited amount we can learn from the same group of people. In fact, without new and different exposures we all tend to become parochial in our thinking and behavior.

The concepts in this book are aimed at interjecting another way of looking at business writing and speaking. Some may seem overly simplified and others bring on a "Hey, that sounds good, I am going to try it!" reaction. This is the target—to get people thinking and to try some simple techniques that work.

Every technique is not going to work well for everyone. People have their own style and some things will fit and others will not. The reader should test those concepts that best fit his or her style. If you find just a few new things that work for you, you are ahead of the game.

Let's face it most of us know we want to write better memos and give better business speeches. Most people have this desire or they would not be reading this right now. The intent is to provide a broad range of possible improvements. Those that don't have value to you should be passed over, but those that fit your style should be tested. If even a few improvements are made, something has been accomplished.

Good luck, and best wishes for success in your business writing and speaking.

RICHARD A. KAUMEYER, JR.
Canoga Park, California

Contents

HOW TO WRITE AND SPEAK IN BUSINESS

1
Business Communications

What are communications? If there is an answer to this question it is a complex one. Most large libraries have hundreds if not thousands of books on the topic. Most universities have multiple courses with "communications" as part of their title, and many offer a major in the subject.

Looking up the term in a dictionary also provides some insight into how broad a field we are dealing with. One will find definitions such as "passing along" or "transferring" information, "giving information via talking, writing, etc." All very broad indeed.

BUSINESS ASPECTS OF COMMUNICATIONS

The intent of this book is to focus on one aspect of the very broad subject of communications; that is, the aspect that affects the business world, in particular, speaking and writing in business. Even with these limitations, the topic is broad and far-reaching.

The intent is not to tackle it from all aspects, nor to delve into a great deal of theory, but to provide those in business with a number of practical techniques and concepts that will help the individual in his or her speaking and writing in a business environment. The techniques are not theoretical, but ones that have been proven effective in actual daily use.

One of the first steps in this process might be to take a step back and ask, "Why do we communicate in business?" If we were to ask this in a group of ten people and make a list we would probably fill several pages on a flipchart or have numerous entries on a blackboard. Figure 1.1 points out only a few of the many answers we will get. Many people have varied ideas as to why we communicate in business, hence the

1. To promote our product.
2. Get information from others.
3. Give direction to my people.
4. Answer my bosses questions.
5. Find out what the customer wants.
6. Obtain direction for planning.
7. Share what is happening.
8. To be part of the group.
9. Find out what others think.
10. To get my job done.

Figure 1.1. Why Do We Communicate In Business?

large number of entries. For our purposes it might be best to try to zero in on the single most important or practical reason people are together in a business environment.

Most people are working at their jobs for economic reasons. This statement will probably draw criticism; for example, there are those who will say that people work to be fulfilled. We have all read the various studies of the reasons people work other than to satisfy economic needs.

These reasons are all valid, possibly, in various contexts, but we agreed earlier that the focus of this book would be practical. So let's try an experiment. Suppose for a minute we gave every one who worked in a particular organization $2 million. How many would be back to work the following Monday, or even the next day? Probably less than five percent would return, if any at all. Consequently, we probably can agree that once most people have satisfied their economic needs, they wouldn't continue in their present work environment.

That is not to say that people will stop working, but once their economic needs are satisfied they will move on to doing what they would truly like to do. However, it is a fact that most people are trapped in their present business environment by their economic needs or lack of financial security.

Money is a measure of value. The next question that might be posed is this: Why do organizations pay people? It appears they do this in order to have them give up what they really want to be doing to perform the task or tasks that the organization wants done.

If we use these concepts then we can focus on a narrower aspect of communication. If people are in organizations to perform tasks in exchange for money, then a large, though not necessarily the whole, of their communications' efforts are probably related to doing just this—trying to accomplish the task or tasks.

HOW DOES BUSINESS COMMUNICATION DIFFER

Look through your memo or letter file, review your daily meeting calendar for the last month, or, if you keep one, review your phone log for a similar period. Most of us will find a pattern. Our efforts at communication have a rather narrow scope in the business world. We spend most of our communications time trying to get a specific task or set of tasks accomplished.

This is going to be a major target of this book. We will focus on the end product of our speaking and writing activities—the accomplishing of tasks. To this end we are going to be rather narrow or parochial, but if we accept this focus, business communication can be improved. Our aim is to get things done with the least amount of effort and then move on to the next task.

COMMUNICATION WITH LEVELS

Most organizations tend to be made up of levels as noted in Figure 1.2. There are certain socially accepted rules and standards of dealing with the various levels. Frequently, these are determined by the nature of the industry and by the corporate culture of the individual organization itself.

Certain organizations will require that communication up and down the organization adhere strictly to the chain of command. Other organizations will be more open and informal; for example, those at the worker level may be invited to have contact with middle- or senior-level management.

As an individual is entering a new organization, or just reviewing the concept of communication in his or her existing organization, it is important to recognize this tone and identify it accurately, because this is one of the first steps toward making effective communication possible. This corporate culture is important; communication practices that may be openly accepted with one organization may be strictly

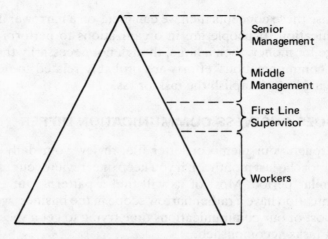

Figure 1.2. Traditional Organization Pyramid.

taboo in another. Quickly learning about the nature of this corporate culture helps an employee avoid embarrassment and the disaster of making a wrong first impression.

Rituals within an organization will vary. Some people are formal and want to be called by their titles; others prefer Mr. or Ms, or within the United States, prefer to be on a first-name basis—the latter being contrary to what is often seen *outside* of the United States. These are all-important concepts to recognize and learn.

An organization's formal structure does not necessarily control the communication structure. There is always an informal line of communications. This exists in all organizations, including those where the formal chain of command is both practiced and effective. This informal network has various names—some refer to it as the "hidden organization" others use the common descriptive term *grapevine*. This is shown in Figure 1.3.

The mistake many people make is in not recognizing the importance of the informal organization structure. Some assume that the official chain of command is the only means of communication; nothing could be more inaccurate.

Even within the formal organization structure communication is not strictly on an up and down path. There is also communication sideways and to other people both higher and lower in the organization in different parts of the structure. This is shown in Figure 1.4.

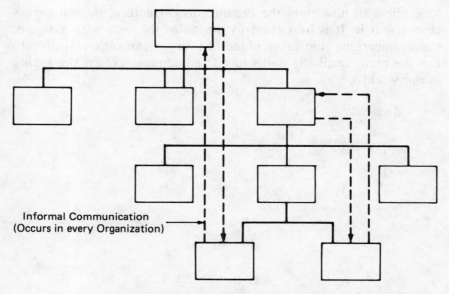

Informal Communication
(Occurs in every Organization)

Figure 1.3. Hidden Organization.

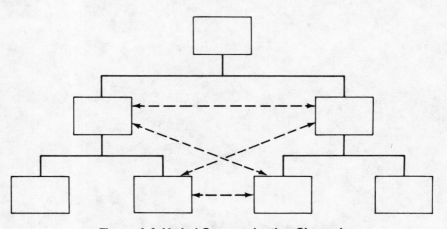

Figure 1.4. Varied Communication Channels.

Regardless of how rigid the organization structure, people always circumvent it. It is important to recognize the very wide range of communications that takes place in every organization, if only to use the many available paths to our advantage. This is the reality of our world.

2
Staff Meetings

The first thing we need to do is define what is meant by a staff meeting. For our purposes, let's define it as a regular meeting between a superior and his or her immediate subordinates. It should consist of everyone who reports to a specific individual. A hypothetical organization chart is shown in Figure 2.1. This shows the groups that would normally make up a staff meeting.

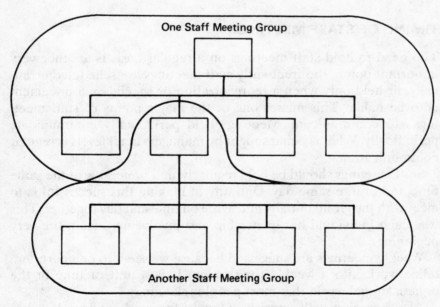

Figure 2.1. Staff Meeting Groupings.

THE KEY TO STAFF MEETINGS

The key to this is very simple—it is a meeting of the supervisor and those he or she supervises. In certain cases it may include staff people or others that the group may feel will make an ongoing contribution, but these exceptions are normally limited. Usually, the number of people an individual manager supervises is relatively small, if the organization structure is well designed. This keeps the staff meeting small and efficient.

What about a person who has only one or two people reporting to them? In this case the staff meeting concept still works. The supervisor or manager should arrange to meet with these people on a regular basis.

Some people find it advantageous to hold meetings at which an entire department is present. As long as the department is small, say five or six people, this may be beneficial. However, as growth occurs the staff meeting benefits are reduced. The concepts noted here work best for a small group with the supervisor and the immediate subordinates involved.

TIMING OF STAFF MEETINGS

The need to hold staff meetings on a regular basis is another very important point. Too frequently staff meetings are scheduled erratically, or held only when a reorganization or special announcement is to be made. This misses one of the major points of staff meetings—to communicate. Meetings held periodically communicate periodically. What is being sought by managers at all levels is regular communication.

Staff meetings should be held regularly, and preferably at the same time and on the same day. One way of making this successful is to meet with the group initially and agree on time and day together. This way each individual has ownership and involvement from the very beginning.

Weekly meetings are suggested because we seem to compartmentalize work into a weekly time frame. It is a unit of time in the organizational world that most people relate to.

Also, a week usually consists of four or five working days. It would seem logical that no superior or subordinate would want to let a longer time frame pass without having some detailed and in-depth communication.

Scheduling the meeting weekly at a specific time assures that people won't forget it or schedule other activities. If everyone agrees that Monday at 3:00 P.M. or Thursday at 9:00 A.M. will be staff meeting time, other events will get scheduled around this. Even if someone is away from their calendar or in another office, when asked for an appointment time they will remember a regularly scheduled staff meeting and not schedule a conflicting event.

WHAT ABOUT ABSENCES

In this busy world of work many people travel, people get ill, take vacations, etc. Do we reschedule the staff meeting? The answer is *"No!"* and it has to be *"No!"* under all circumstances. The staff meeting must be held if there is only one person left and "they have to sit and talk to themselves." This, of course, is an exaggeration for emphasis.

The point is that it is important that everyone knows the staff meeting will be held as scheduled. Once it is canceled, it is easy to cancel again. To prevent this from happening, therefore, it is important to have a line of succession for the leadership. If the superior is absent due to travel or illness, then a substitute from the group should be identified to take over. If the substitute is absent, then a third alternate designated, then a fourth, and so on.

It is important to decide the alternates who will lead the staff meeting before the need arises. We might have the group involved in this planning session in the same manner we had them involved in deciding the meeting time. This method furthers team building and gives individuals ownership in the group.

SETTING OF STAFF MEETINGS

Some superiors hold staff meetings in their offices, other have a "stand-up meeting" in the work area, etc. Neither of these alternatives is ideal; the most effective method is to have the meeting in a separate conference room with a circular table or seating arrangement.

Interruptions should not be allowed; coffee or refreshments should be provided; a chalkboard or flipchart should be handy at all times.

The major point in preparing the meeting is to assure that all external stimuli or distractions are avoided. There is really very little occurring in an organization that is as important as the staff meeting while it is in process. The time without interruptions should be jealously guarded. This is a concept that may take some time to become firmly established in an organization.

Holding the staff meeting away from the immediate office area, if possible, signals to others that it has importance. The fact that the group involved has gone into a conference room rather than staying in the immediate work area gives the meeting an air of formality. If the organization's physical facilities allow for this, it has a definite advantage.

However, the fact that a conference room does not exist or is not available at the time the meeting is scheduled should not become an excuse for canceling it. The staff meeting should be held regardless. The act of the meeting itself is far more important than the available facilities. Try for a conference room, but if one is not available, hold the regular meeting in the nearest available facility.

ORGANIZATION OF STAFF MEETING

The staff meeting a supervisor holds with his or her subordinates is probably the most important staff meeting that exists in an organization. This extends all the way from the meetings held by first-line supervisors with their staffs, through those held by the chairman with the board of directors. These meetings all provide three important inputs to the organization: education of the members, communication within the group, and problem solving. This is shown in Figure 2.2. It might be said that these functions dictate the structure of the meeting. To achieve the three inputs noted, the meeting format must be geared to these aims.

There are probably multiple meeting formats that can produce the desired results. One that has proven effective will be discussed here. This assumes that the meeting is regularly scheduled—preferably weekly on the same day, starting always at the same time and on time, and in the same location if possible.

The agenda for the meeting should be sent out ahead of time whenever possible. A sample agenda is shown in Figure 2.3. This allows each member to have some advance idea regarding what the

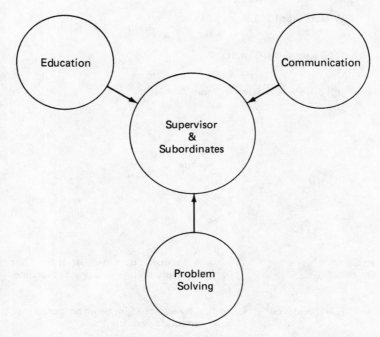

Figure 2.2. Why Staff Meetings Are "The Most Important Meeting."

meeting will cover. It should spell out not only where and when the meeting will be held, but provide enough details on items to be discussed so that members can fully prepare themselves. This can help cut back on the number of unresolved issues that must be carried to the next meeting.

This is an important concept. Members should not arrive at the meeting and be greeted by surprises. If they are to participate intelligently, they need advance information on what will be covered. It is important that the agenda provide sufficient details to allow this to occur.

In some cases, advance copies of the reports, forms, etc., should accompany the agenda. This is particularly important if a decision must be reached or comments solicited. No one can plow through pages of documentation and give a well-thought out decision on the spur of the moment without preparation time.

In addition to an agenda, minutes should be taken if at all possible, and a formal minute file maintained. This assures not only that

Date: Week of April 1, 198_

Time: 8:00 a.m. to 11:00 a.m.

Location: 9th Floor — Conference Room A

Agenda

Item	Detail
1. Guest Speaker R. Smith	A discussion by a member of local phone company on new equipment available.
2. Film — "Safety and You"	A new safety film being proposed for corporate wide use.
3. Roundtable	Update by each member of items happening in their area.

Figure 2.3.
Sample Agenda
Administrative Department

decisions are recorded but that there is a record of the means by which they were arrived at. It is usually a good idea to have the same person take the minutes each week. This allows a format and style to develop with which the group can become familiar. There is an art to listening and taking minutes that takes time to develop. The person assigned to the task will grow with it, and usually the product (minutes) will improve over time.

A copy of the minutes in draft form should be circulated to attendees prior to finalization. This assures that the true meaning was actually captured. When finalized the minutes should be distributed again to each member. This reinforces the importance of the staff meeting and what was done there. The minutes are a product or output of the meeting. They represent an accomplishment to those participating as well as a record regarding what was done.

STAFF MEETING PROCEDURE

People or events with specific schedules should start off the meeting; for example, the guest speakers, films, etc. This is in contrast to individual staff meeting member presentations which may be more open ended in terms of time. Staff meetings should be set up to allow discussion of concerns, problems, etc., that individual members may have. There should always be time left open at the end of the meeting so that these can occur.

Generally, if it is anticipated that the staff meeting will be two hours, allow for three. Have everyone block this out on their calendar. If less time is needed and the meeting adjourns early, members are usually happy and can find use for the additional time. They are in a bind, however, if they plan for only two hours and really need three hours.

This does not mean that the members can assume they have unlimited time and can rattle on forever. Time control is one of the roles of the leader. If there are six members, each should be advised of, say, a ten-minute time allotment. If a member starts to run over, the leader may want to ask the person to summarize. If a heated discussion has arisen, the leader may wish to poll the group as to whether they wish to continue when the time allotment runs out.

One important facet of each staff meeting is that a roundtable or round robin type opportunity should occur. The leader should go to each member in turn and ask about comments regarding their area of responsibility.

IMPORTANCE OF ROUNDTABLE DISCUSSION

The importance of going around the group and having a roundtable discussion can't be stressed enough. It is the single most important aspect of the staff meeting. You might even call it the heart or core of the staff meeting. It is the activity that makes the staff meeting the most important meeting held in an organization.

Everyone likes to think that this meeting or that meeting is the most important one. In individual instances they can probably fully justify their point. However, the staff meeting is the building block for all other meetings. This is where ideas are discussed in their embryonic stage and developed. Without good staff meetings throughout an organization, true potential for that organization will not be achieved.

Within this framework of importance, the roundtable discussion becomes very significant because it facilitates the three targets we identified earlier—education, communication, and problem solving.

Now let's go into this in some detail. Figure 2.4 depicts pictorially the value of going around the group. Each of the items noted contribute to the success and value of the staff meeting.

Shared Pressure

Many supervisors and managers hesitate to hold staff meetings, not for time reasons as they often indicate, but because of fear of not knowing how to run a meeting or fear that they can't control it. Using the group process greatly alleviates many of these fears and pressures.

It simplifies the staff meeting process and gives everyone ownership in making it work. This becomes the body of the staff meeting or the main portion of the staff meeting. The leader does not do all of the talking, but has each member participate.

Usually the leader shares four or five items of significance that are occurring in the department or organization. For example, a brief statement about performance appraisals and the due date for the department, possibly some comments on the recent merger, an overview of what was accomplished at the last sales review, etc. He or she will limit themselves to the time agreed upon, say five or ten minutes.

Then the leader will turn to the next person at the table and say something like "Mary what is new in your area?" This will go on until everyone has shared what is happening in their area.

The first couple of times it is just a brief "show and tell," and then

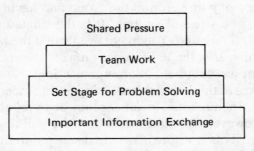

Figure 2.4. Value of Going Around the Group "Roundtable Discussion."

people start to bring in and interject problems, concerns, major issues, etc. The leader does not have to spend hours in preparation to have a successful meeting at this stage because the responsibility for preparation has been distributed or shared, as has the pressure. Each member now has a responsibility and an ownership role in the staff meeting.

TEAM WORK

There is a certain psychological bond that people achieve when they get together as a group. This shared experience tends to bring people closer together. It might be called a membership bonding.

The surprising thing is how quickly this can happen. Many people have recognized this in the strong supportive feeling that occurs in just attending a three- or four-day seminar. In fact, many people feel an air of sadness when the seminar is over. It is like having to say good-bye to family or old friends, yet you have known the people in the group for a very short period of time.

The same effect can be valuable to any supervisor if channeled properly. One of the elements of leadership is to bring the group together as a team. Regular staff meetings definitely set the stage and provide the environment to do this.

INFORMATION EXCHANGE

Those people reporting to the supervisor or manager holding the staff meeting are the supposed members of the staff meeting. Normally, they would have to be in related areas to have such a reporting relationship. This means that they deal with issues of mutual interest.

In day-to-day activities often we don't take the time to exchange needed information with our work peers. Usually, information is exchanged on a crisis basis. A problem or issue becomes so big that we get together and exchange information in an effort to solve it.

Staff meetings certainly do not stop all crisis-related information exchanges. However, they do prevent some of them. If you don't believe this, observe the group dynamics at the next staff meeting you attend. Most significant points will be discussed during the roundtable discussion.

The actual need for specific information and its exchange becomes

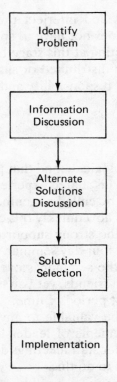

Figure 2.5. Problem Solving Phases.

very obvious. Mary will be explaining what has been happening in her area. Someone, say Joe, will stop her to ask a series of questions. Mary will answer and provide more detail as indicated by the questions. June may even muse out loud on how the information Mary has given may impact on XYZ project. She may chime in that she sees a new approach based on what Mary has said and Joe's comments. In this case, information has been exchanged and possibly even further synthesized based on the input from other members. This probably would not have happened without the regularly scheduled staff meeting.

PROBLEM SOLVING

Staff meetings tend to set the stage for problem solving if only because the leader of a specific area is present with the people that report to him or her. Issues are being presented and information exchanged. These are certainly the ingredients with which to bring problems to the surface.

As noted in Figure 2.5, the ingredients are there also to solve the problems that surface. When the group identifies the problem that surfaced, they have a forum for discussion readily available. The people familiar with the work environment usually will be present, so alternate solutions can be discussed and a solution selected and implemented.

Of course, problems will surface that are outside the scope of the staff meeting group so that they won't be able to go through the steps listed in Figure 2.5. However, most people are surprised at the large number of problems in this group that come up and are within its scope and receive instant attention.

There are so many, in fact, that many find a staff meeting group to be a problem-solving team. It makes one wonder what happens where staff meetings aren't held. Do these problems just fester and become crises? Is this why so many organizations spend their time in one state of crisis management or another fighting fires?

No value judgment on the relationship between organizations not having staff meetings and the number of crises will be drawn here. However, it is certainly food for thought.

3
Large Group Meetings

The definition of what constitutes a large group can be a problem in itself. What is a large group to one person may be a small group to another, and vice versa.

A hundred people can be a small group to a person who is used to audiences of several thousand. At the same time, some people experience stage fright in a conversation with three or more people. Obviously, we have a problem in that the definition varies from person to person.

BUSINESS DEFINITION

Let's try to develop a definition for our purposes. Most managers limit the number of people they have reporting to them to around five or seven as the maximum. The term used to describe this is *span of control.*

Of course, as with any numerical statement one can immediately conjure up all sorts of exceptions. There are some managers who have only one person reporting to them, and others who have fifteen.

Almost everyone in business knows the standard jokes that are exchanged regarding committees—usually large ones. One often hears comments such as these: "If you don't want any action taken, assign it to a committee!" or "A camel is a horse designed by a committee."

The interesting thing is that it is hard to find an organization that does not have committees of all sizes, shapes, and varieties. It is doubtful that they would exist if they didn't fulfill a purpose.

When asked, most managers will respond that if you get past seven to ten people you don't get much done. There seems to be almost universal agreement that a working or productive committee is around this number. Yet, all of us know committees in our own as well as other organizations that are greater in size than this magic seven to ten number.

The fact that such a number exists may help us in understanding two things. First, if we consider the concept of maximum span of control or the number of people most people have reporting to them, and then couple this with what most managers feel is an effective working group or committee, we have a rough number for a small group. This is depicted in Figure 3.1. In a business sense these seem to be the numbers most people feel constitute a small and effective, productive group.

Most managers seem to feel they are dealing with large groups once group size exceeds ten. For our purposes this may be a good point at which to divide large groups from small ones. Whether we like it or not, agree or disagree with the definition, this is where most businesses seem to draw the dividing line in everyday practice. All one has to do is to observe any organization in daily operation.

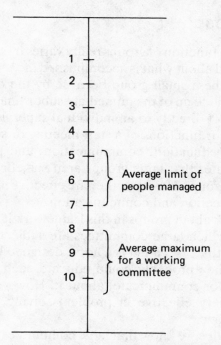

Figure 3.1. Groups Small Enough to Be Productive.

In addition to this size break that provides us with a definition of group size, a very interesting question is also raised. If groups larger than ten are joked about, often not considered productive, referred to as ineffective, etc., why do they exist? Because the fact is, not only do they exist, but there is no indication they are ever going to go away. Look at any large organization and you will see that large groups proliferate.

The obvious point is they produce some benefit or they would not continue. The real issue that will be developed in this chapter is that large groups have a function and purpose. This function and purpose is similar to that of a small group, yet very different in major essentials. Understanding this difference will help us to know when a small group is appropriate and when a large group is to be used. It seems it is the misunderstanding and misuse of groups that leads to the jokes and the discussion of productivity and effectiveness. Using the wrong group size to perform a specific task seems to result in the task not being accomplished.

GROUP PURPOSE

The purpose and function of groups really varies by size. In a previous chapter we talked about what is accomplished in a staff meeting. This would normally be a small group because by the definition we are using here, it is made up of the immediate subordinates; that is, those people who report directly to an individual supervisor or manager.

The three major functions of a staff meeting or small group listed previously were education, communication, and problem solving. Figure 3.2 indicates that large groups aren't as effective at problem solving as small groups. However, they are effective in dealing with the functions of education and communication.

When we think about groups in this framework it explains some of the ridicule to which large committees are subject. The previously mentioned joke that, "A camel is a horse designed by a committee," makes sense. They probably could educate each other about the horse, and talk (or communicate) about it. However, they probably would not be very effective in problem solving, or in this case, designing the horse.

In actual practice we know that large committees and other groups of size are given problems to solve. Some, contrary to what we have been saying, do a rather good job of problem solving despite all the

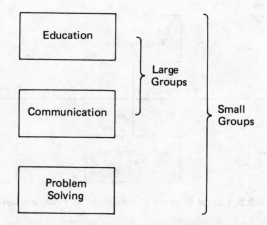

Figure 3.2. Functions a Group May Perform.

jokes that we hear. If one observes an effective committee or large group that is good at dealing with problems, we seem to find a pattern. Either formally or informally the group is breaking down into small groups, usually task forces, subcommittees, study teams, design teams, etc.

Figure 3.3 depicts this activity. The problems are actually worked on by smaller groups that are usually more effective at problem solving activity than a large group would be.

FORMAL REPORTING

If we focus on the activities of large groups, one item will stand out above all others. This is the method of reporting to the main body or group; it is shown in Figure 3.4

The reason for this centers on the major function of large groups which is education and communication. To achieve this, they must have a way of knowing what is going on. Much of the real problem solving (some would say productive activity) is occurring in the task forces and subcommittees. They have the charter or responsibility to get back to the main group with what they found out.

The information exchange, as noted in Figure 3.5 is lengthened in a large-group environment. There is frequently a filter or middleman between the information and the large group; for example, the subcommittee, task force, etc.

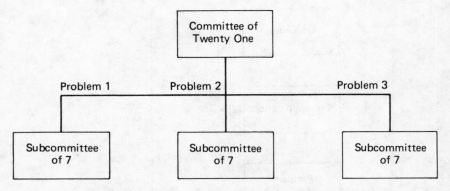

Figure 3.3. Large Groups Successful at Problem Solving.

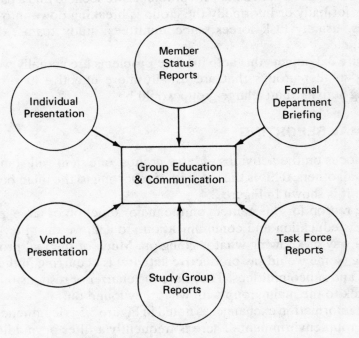

Figure 3.4. Large Group Formal Reporting.

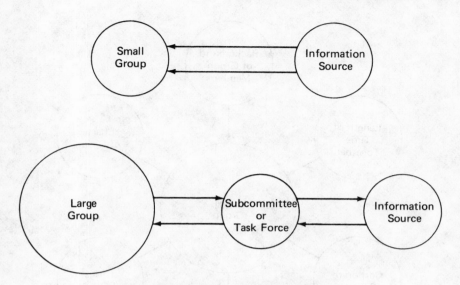

Figure 3.5. Information Exchange.

NEED TO ESTABLISH WORKING RELATIONSHIPS

By their very nature, small groups can operate on an informal basis. Problem situations can be discussed and resolved on the spot. People quickly develop working relationships and learn to anticipate one another's reactions.

There are many factors that influence the working relationships in a large group, a few of which are shown in Figure 3.6. This is not to say that the same factors don't impact on small groups; but sheer size causes the factors to magnify in importance.

Let's look at a few of these factors and how they impact on the group's position within the organization. (It must be remembered that the target audience is business and its environment.) The charter of the group is an important factor in its ability to interact. Why the group was set up, and what areas it has authority to act in are important elements. If it is a finance committee, then the group as a whole or its subcommittees/task forces probably will have access to any and all financial data—regardless of whether confidential or not. However, if it were an employee suggestions committee it probably would not have access to financial data.

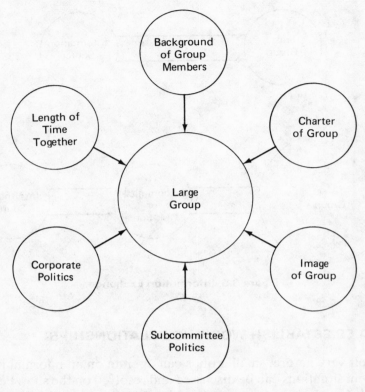

Figure 3.6. Influences on Working Relationships.

The image of the committee is another factor. Who set it up and why may be a very important factor in determining how a committee functions. Obviously, if the committee was set up at the direction and reports to the chairman of the board, it will have more authority than if its mentor were the manager of administration.

Subcommittee politics will have an influence on the internal working relationships. If early on the members of the groups develop good working relationships, often this will carry on into the functioning of the subcommittees. However, if there is a great deal of jealousy and competition between individuals, problems frequently result and free exchange of information and open assistance in problem solving do not develop. These interpersonal problems become deterrents to the smooth-functioning of the communication process.

Corporate policies can also influence the working relationship. If, for example, the president of the firm is at odds with the executive vice president who is in charge of the finance committee this will impact the committee's activities. The knowledge that there is an outside conflict may strongly affect how the group thinks and the action it takes, or doesn't take.

The length of time the group has been together also influences the working relationships. Groups take time to grow and evolve. They go through stages leading to maturity almost as human beings do. Those groups that have been together for a longer period of time will normally share a level of maturity not found with a new group.

The background of the group members can also influence the working relationship within and outside of the group. Strong leaders with a reputation for accomplishment will have contacts and access to resources. These attributes can impact on how the group is perceived, its acceptance, and its ability to perform.

4
Individual Meetings

Probably no topic is written about more than communication between individuals. It is discussed in every aspect from one-way communication, such as giving orders, to the more common two-way communications shown in Figure 4.1. All of us are engaged in communication with individuals on a regular and one-on-one basis. The business world is no exception. In fact, by its very nature business provides an environment where we probably see the greatest amount of individual meetings; for example, to request supplies, for counseling sessions, or to describe needed repairs, etc. The instrument most used in business, the telephone, was developed to facilitate the need to communicate one to one.

INDIVIDUAL STYLE

Very few people are truly effective in business unless they have developed the ability successfully to conduct meetings with individuals. We all hear the tales about the successful executive who only will communicate by memo, or the one who is good with large groups but not on a one-on-one basis.

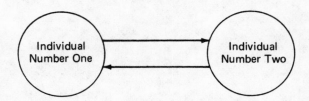

Figure 4.1. Individual Communication. As the arrows indicate, it is usually a two-way street.

One wonders if that is not what these are—tales and possibly fairy tales—based on imagination or fantasy? How many successful executives, managers, supervisors, businessmen, or businesswomen, do you know who aren't good in a one-on-one situation? In fact, if we think about it, using the concept of those who are successful, we find that such people usually possess outstanding skills in this area.

People who are tonguetied, shy, those who don't relate well with people, usually aren't successful in business. Sure, we can all pick examples of someone who is not strong in this area who has had a successful career, but such people are rare. Think of those you know who are poor in this area, but successful. You can probably count them on one hand.

There is a correlation between success and the ability to communicate. There is also a strong and obvious connection between being successful and being able to communicate on a one-on-one basis, if for no other reason than because so much of this type of communication occurs in business.

HOW DO YOU KNOW WHETHER YOU'RE A STRONG/WEAK COMMUNICATOR?

This is an interesting area: Are you strong or weak in communicating with another individual? Left to make our own evaluation most of us would rate ourselves high. But is this true? We all have a blind spot where our own weaknesses are concerned. It is human nature to rate ourselves higher than we are.

If we rate ourselves high in individual communication, but are in fact weak in this area, we are programming ourselves for failure. How do we achieve the necessary input as to our strengths and weaknesses in this aspect of communication?

One way is to ask others what they think. In fact, if we are weak in this area it may already have come out in a performance review. However, asking others you work with assumes several factors: that they are honest and open about telling us the truth about ourselves; and that they are qualified to make the judgment we are asking them to make.

Probably the most effective way to find out our skills is this area is through the use of an outside consultant. More and more we are finding small- and middle-sized firms that have skilled management consultants on retainer. This used to be a luxury only utilized by large conglomerates. But today, most organizations, large and small, recognize that things are changing so rapidly that they need qualified outside advice in order to make sure that employees' communications skills keep pace with these changes.

It is wise to avail ourselves of this resource. Each of us is more effective if we have a realistic understanding of our strengths and weaknesses. Those blind spots we discussed earlier can be dangerous. Using an outside expert gives us feedback in this area that can be invaluable to a person's career.

COMMUNICATION AUDIT

Each of us can benefit from a "communication audit" of our abilities in this area. Taking away all of the masks and other blocks, how do we communicate with other individuals in the business environment? A good audit should focus on all aspects of our normal business relationships. As shown in Figure 4.2, these include superiors, peers, and subordinates.

The aim is to identify problems or weak spots with individual communication skills. Almost everyone we deal with in a business environment, inside or outside of a firm, fits into the categories listed. They are either at a higher level, an equivalent level, or a lower level.

Breaking the audit into these groups may be useful for several reasons. It gives us more than one focus and recognizes that people vary in individual communication skills with different levels of people. All of us know of managers who are great at communicating with their superiors, but not good at communicating with individual subordinates. Some may say, "This is true, but they still seem to get the job done, why do they need to change?" The basic answer is in order to be more effective! If individual communication is weak in any area, the person is not working at maximum effectiveness.

IMPROVING SKILLS

Once the consultant has done an audit on an employee, a weak area may well have been discovered. For instance, the person may have poor listening and counseling skills when dealing with subordinates. What happens next?

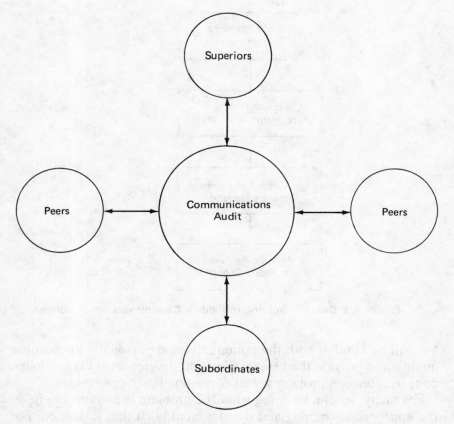

Figure 4.2. Focus Of Individual Communications Audit.

One immediate benefit is that the person has been informed that a weakness exists. The simple act of consciousness raising can provide some immediate benefits. The old saying "knowledge is power" applies here. Having a blind spot regarding an area that needs improving does not act to anyone's benefit.

Now that the problem is identified, what are the steps involved to deal with or solve it? Figure 4.3 indicates these steps. The first step after the consciousness-raising stage would be to take some positive action.

Training and development in the area where more strength is needed will provide positive and practical assistance. A good consulting resource will not only be able to identify the individual's weaknesses,

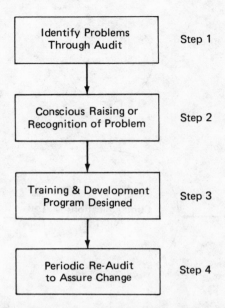

Figure 4.3. Steps In Solving Individual Communication Problems.

but will be familiar with the community and personally know those qualified to provide the best training and development via seminars, college extension programs, and correspondence courses.

For many people, knowing what the problem is and zeroing in on the appropriate training and development is all that is needed. For others, it may take substantially more effort to produce the necessary changes. The real challenge is to make certain that the improvement is both real and lasting.

The situation should be reaudited after six months, and again in a year after the training and development program is completed. This is to assure that the desired set of skills has been acquired by the individual on a lasting basis rather than being a cosmetic or temporary improvement.

BASIC TIPS

Whether or not you choose to have a professional audit and obtain any specific training and development, there are some basic methods that will improve the communications' level of meetings with individuals. Many of these hints are just commonsense items that we can overlook. Putting them into practice can show immediate results.

Planning

No one would make a major address before a crowded auditorium without major preparation because all want to be successful in making our points and gain the respect of the audience.

Unfortunately, many of us hold individual meetings with our staff, peers, and superiors without any preparation. Obviously we cannot always prepare if the meeting is on the spur of the moment, or the other person has requested it and we don't know much about the topic. However, if we review the meetings that we have throughout the day normally we have time to prepare and either know the topic or can find out about it beforehand.

In the case of meetings that we set up and schedule, we always have control—though too often we don't do our homework. The meeting starts in a rambling fashion, some topics to be discussed are forgotten, decisions are not made, and so on. The meeting is held, but its productivity is questionable.

We can control this problem by proper planning. Items to be discussed should be jotted on a piece of paper. It can be dangerous to rely on memory. Some people make notes on their calendar beside the date and time they are meeting with a specific individual. Others keep a pad with brief topic notes they wish to discuss. An example is shown in Figure 4.4.

As seen in the example, these notes don't have to be detailed. Usually, just short "bullets" to remind us of topics to be discussed are sufficient. The list is usually "additive" and should be kept handy; that is, we frequently think of other things to discuss with the person after arranging the meeting and before it occurs.

If, for example, we set up a Wednesday meeting with Joe Jones on Monday we may have only one original topic to discuss. However, before the meeting takes place several other items may come up that would be more appropriate to discuss. In this case it is easy to add them to the list before they are forgotten. It is a simple technique that frequently improves one's individual communication ability by several percentage points.

Don't be afraid to have your list with you, or right in front of you,

<u>July 27th</u>

10:00 a.m.	Meeting S. Miller — Status of project Y — Approval to add three people to staff — His view of last week's staff meeting.
2:00 p.m.	Meeting J. Jones — Ask for copy of budget — Evaluation of current applicant search.

<u>July 28th</u>

9:00 a.m.	Meeting R. Roberts — Review project X — Department vacation-schedule

Figure 4.4. Informal Meeting Notes

when talking to the other individual. It shows you are organized and respect the other person's time and indeed this will serve to enhance your image. Almost everyone hates nonproductive or wandering meetings.

Office Barriers

The work desk can often be a barrier between you and the other individual. Sitting behind it when dealing with another individual signals a very formal message. In essence it says that you want a formal mood and the person kept at a distance. If this is the type of environment desired, that is fine, but it is important to recognize that it exists.

If you are seeking a favor, trying to obtain more open and honest responses, or wish to establish a friendship or comradery it might be better to get away from the desk. Try to arrange your office so that side chairs are available. Then, if you wish, you can get up from the desk and join the person in one of these chairs. This eliminates the "desk barrier" between you.

If an office is not available and you are using a small conference room, the table may become a barrier. This is easily remedied by joining the person on the same side of the table. Sometimes you may wish to pull two chairs to the side in an open space in the room, to further assure that barriers don't exist.

Relieving Tension

For thousands of years many have recognized that business communication seems to improve when the atmosphere is less tense. This is particularly true if one person is trying to convince another of the merits of a particular position, product, service, and so on.

There are some people who are naturally effective at doing this. Possibly this is part of the concept of charisma. These gifted few can charm people and create a relaxing atmosphere almost anywhere. Then there are the rest of us, normal mortals, who need help in doing this.

Let's face it, the office environment is not conducive to releasing tension. In fact, it can create tension. We are at the mercy of the emergency phone call, the knock at the door with an urgent message, etc. Is it any wonder that more business is said to be conducted during a golf game or over lunch than in the office? As shown in Figure 4.5, such social occasions bridge the communication barrier.

Of course, business lunches (sometimes referred to as the three-martini lunch) are much maligned. However, they continue, and are encouraged by even the most dollar-conscious corporations. They are probably the mainstay of the banking and financial industry.

Timing is the secret of effective use of the business lunch. Normally, the tension is at its height at the beginning of lunch. This can be attributed to a whole host of reasons—a busy morning with many problems, unfamiliar surroundings in the restaurant, hunger, low blood sugar before eating, wondering what the other person wants, etc.

So, if you have a major point to make, the beginning of the lunch is probably not the best time to make it. By the same token, you don't want your companion to spend all the lunch wondering what you are going to drop on them. A happy medium has to be reached. Possibly a broad outline of the area you want to talk about, or a minor item on

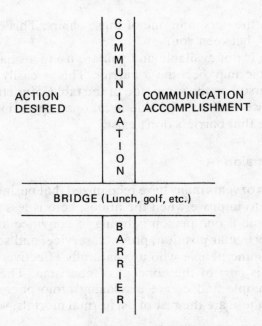

Figure 4.5. Bridging the Communication Barrier.

your agenda should be addressed at the beginning of the lunch. As shown in Figure 4.6, the real benefits of communication and achievement are normally going to occur near the end of the meeting. This is the point at which to zero in on the real purpose of the meeting when people are most often relaxed, comfortable, and ready to listen with interest.

Emotional Individuals

A one-on-one situation that most people fear and try to avoid is dealing with an emotional individual—crying or angry. These are situations everyone faces in the business world. One might say it is an unpleasant fact of life.

There are, however, tricks to handling communication with these individuals. Those in heavy public contact such as personnel, public relations, customer service groups, etc., soon learn some quick and easy methods to deal with the situation.

The one who cries is usually less threatening than the person who is exhibiting terrible anger. Although crying may be a way of releasing

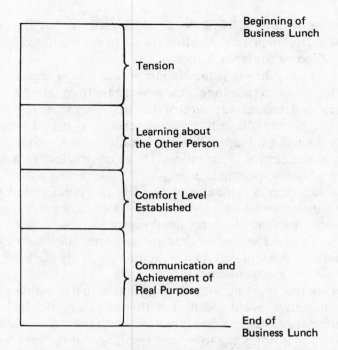

Figure 4.6. Importance of Timing at a Business Lunch.

anger, we are less likely to get punched in the nose or physically assaulted by the one who cries.

Some people loose control and cry while others use it as a deliberate manipulative technique to throw the other person off balance. If possible, try not to problem solve or get into any detailed discussion while the person is out of control. You are at a disadvantage.

In a business situation we are not going to try to play amateur psychologist. Ours is not the role of determining underlying psychological reasons for emotions. Whether the person was improperly toilet trained or hated their mother is not our concern. With this in mind, our aim is to get the person back in control, and see if there is a work-related problem that is causing the distress.

If this is the case, we need to deal with the problem the same as if the person had not been crying. If it isn't work related then the person should be referred to their clergy or their physician. Some corporations have an employee assistance function that may be able to provide counsel.

Again, our aim is to stop the crying and find out if there is a work-related problem. How do we deal with this? If the outburst hasn't occurred in private, the first step is to get the individual into a private office or conference room.

The best thing to say is nothing until the person regains control. Gently tell them to take their time and regain their composure. Stay with them for a reasonable period of time until they regain control—say five or ten minutes. Briefly try to determine if it is a personal or business-related problem. Personal problems may require special additional concern and attention. Don't try to discuss a business problem while the person is crying.

If the situation continues and there is every indication you are dealing with someone who has a work-related concern, suggest they come back when they have regained their composure. Set a specific time to meet with them while they are with you, later that day, or the following day. You will find this rescheduling usually works well and is appreciated by everyone involved.

A one-on-one meeting with an angry individual is another type we would all rather avoid. Although this situation rarely becomes physically dangerous, at times it can be. Until the individual is under control, there is not going to be any resolution of the problem.

Suppose someone shows up at your office door. They are red in the face, yelling, apparently very angry about the processing of their order. What do you do? One step is to buy yourself some time. Time will frequently cool at least the violent uncontrolled pattern of anger.

Try to get the person to sit down and find an excuse to leave them alone in your office for a few minutes. If all else fails, tell them you have to go to the bathroom and will be right back. Even the terribly angry seem to understand nature's call. Leave them alone five or ten minutes if possible. This has a remarkable calming effect. If possible have someone offer them a cup of coffee and a magazine while you are away.

When leaving is out of the question, the next best thing to do is to listen attentively. Give the individual a chance to vent their rage. Tell them you can't make any promises, but ask them what action they want you to take. Will they be satisfied if you take a particular line of action? Again, take normal steps in buying time for a cooling-off period. Not easy, but effective.

5
The Memo

Of the vehicles used to communicate in business, the memo has to be near the top of the list with the telephone. Internally many companies even have preprinted headers at the top of memo paper such as the three styles shown in Figure 5.1.

This becomes a standard stock form with the headers preprinted so that a typist doesn't have to repeat them. This indicates heavy usage or volume. In most companies memos almost reach blizzard proportions.

There is a memo sent detailing almost any event or happening. There are memos sent out explaining how to write memos. Others are sent out instructing people to write fewer memos, and so on.

Because of the increasing costs of secretarial help, some firms encourage the use of handwritten memos. A sample of one of these is included in Figure 5.2 (Sample 1). These vary as to style and format. Many have carbons attached so that a file copy is made as the original writing occurs.

Another style is shown in Figure 5.3 (Sample 2). Here a section for a response is added. This becomes what is often referred to as a "turnaround document" because it is used twice or returned. The first time for the inquiry and then later to answer that inquiry.

These forms may also come with various copies included. Some allow one copy for the sender and one for the recipient who will respond. This assures that everyone has a copy in case one is lost in transmittal, or a question arises at a later date regarding what decision or agreement that was arrived at.

If there is a single point to be made in all of this, it is that the memo is a very integral and formalized part of the business world. Few businesses could operate without them. Try as we may, a better

```
+--------------------------------------------------------+
|                      MEMORANDUM                        |
|                                                        |
|   To:                          Date:                   |
|                                                        |
|   From:                                                |
|                                                        |
|   Subject:                                             |
|                                                        |
|                         Sample 1                       |
+--------------------------------------------------------+
```

```
+--------------------------------------------------------+
|                      MEMORANDUM                        |
|                                                        |
|   To:                                                  |
|                                                        |
|   From:                                                |
|                                                        |
|   Subject:                                             |
|                                                        |
|   Date:                                                |
|                                                        |
|                         Sample 2                       |
+--------------------------------------------------------+
```

```
+--------------------------------------------------------+
|                      MEMORANDUM                        |
|                                                        |
|   To:                          Date:                   |
|                                                        |
|   From:                        Subject:                |
|                                                        |
|                         Sample 3                       |
+--------------------------------------------------------+
```

Figure 5.1. Styles of Preprinted Memo Heads.

```
┌─────────────────────────────────────────────────────────────┐
│              MEMORANDUM (Handwritten)                         │
│                                                               │
│  To:_____  Subject:_____   │
│                                                               │
│  From:_____  Date: _____  │
│                                                               │
│  _____    │
│                                                               │
│  _____    │
│                                                               │
│  _____    │
│                                                               │
│  _____    │
│                                                               │
│  _____    │
│                                                               │
│  _____    │
│                                                               │
│  _____    │
│                                                               │
│  _____    │
│                                                               │
│  Signed:                        Date:                         │
│                                                               │
│  _____    │
└─────────────────────────────────────────────────────────────┘
```

Figure 5.2. Handwritten Communications Forms (Sample 1).

substitute has not been found. For this reason it becomes imperative that we learn to effectively use this important management communications tool.

MEMO HATERS

Most of us know people who absolutely hate to write memos. These are the same ones who deny the need for them and refer to them as a waste of time. If they were unneeded and a waste of time, memos would have disappeared from the business scene a long time ago.

```
┌─────────────────────────────────────────────────────────────┐
│                   MEMORANDUM (Handwritten)                    │
│                                                               │
│  To:_____    Subject: _____  │
│  From:_____    Date: _____  │
│                                                               │
│  _____ │
│  _____ │
│  _____ │
│  _____ │
│                                                               │
│  Signed: _____    Date: _____  │
│  _____ │
│                          Response                             │
│  _____ │
│  _____ │
│  _____ │
│  _____ │
│  _____ │
│                                                               │
│  Signed:                       Date:                          │
│  _____ │
└─────────────────────────────────────────────────────────────┘
```

Figure 5.3. Handwritten Communication Form (Sample 2).

They haven't, so they obviously serve a very real purpose. People in business are too pragmatic to continue with a tool that isn't making a bottom line contribution.

If we look a little further we usually find some other reasons for their dislike. One often is that it takes time to write a memo and forces a person to organize their thoughts and feelings about a specific topic.

In essence, a memo forces one to take position or make a commitment. We have all heard the comment that what someone said is only as good as what is in writing. Many people avoid being pinned down. If things change or aren't the way they expected, they want to deny involvement, and let someone else take the blame.

Written records (memos) don't allow this to happen. They document the what, where, why, and when of the situation or requested activities. This is why they are so valuable in getting things done. This is also why many people fear them, since there is little room for denial when the statements are in writing.

However, possibly the major reason people don't like to write memos is that they don't know how to do so. This is very hard for managers and supervisors to admit, since they know consciously or subconsciously how important memos are in the business world. It is much easier for them to downgrade the importance of memos, than to face their own weaknesses in this area.

This is not necessarily the fault of the managers and supervisors. There is actually little or no training in our school system nor in our business organizations on how to set down ideas on paper in an organized and intelligible fashion, which is the essence of writing effective memos. It is just assumed that people know how to do this, but where they learned how to is anyone's guess.

MEMO VERSUS LETTER

It is interesting to note that many people receive instruction early in life on letter writing, thank you letters to aunts, uncles, grandparents, love letters to girl friends/boyfriends, letters home from camp, letters while on military duty, etc.

This type of experience is nice, but probably at odds with what is needed in a memo. Letters are generally newsy or chatty. They ramble on and on about what one has seen or experienced.

If we reflect on this, it is probably the area in which most of us receive our initial writing experience. School compositions and term papers are there, but they have little impact on the real world. Unless you are in an academic working environment it is doubtful you are going to turn in a theme or a term paper to a boss or co-worker.

What you are going to give them most often is a memo. The closest thing to a memo you have ever written is a letter to a friend or relative. Unfortunately, this may be the reason why so many memos sound like letters to Aunt Tillie.

They ramble on all over the barnyard describing people, events, experience, feelings, etc., all of which have absolutely nothing to do with the situation at hand. As can be seen in Figure 5.4, our formal background is usually slim.

BASIC MEMO PARTS

If we focus on the reason for business communication discussed earlier, the concept of memo writing may fall into place. We decided earlier that communication in business took place in order *to accomplish a task*. This definition helps in distinguishing a memo from a letter. A memo has to go right to the heart of the problem.

The memo should be aimed at getting part of that all-important task accomplished. With this as the target, we can take some of the

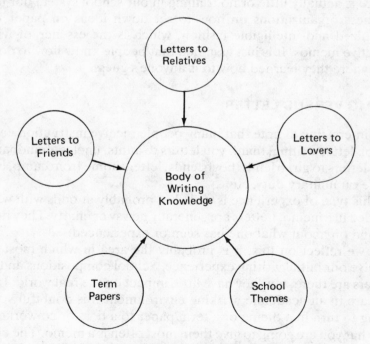

Figure 5.4. Memo Writing Experience.

mystery out of memo writing and even establish a formula that can be used for almost any memo.

Some books go through elaborate steps to point out all the possible parts that can go into a memo. They wind up with six to sixteen points that most of us can't remember. Then we are back to square one.

The formula given here is not going to meet every memo-writing situation. It is imperfect and variations will be required in certain cases. However, if we get the basic steps down, the deviations can be handled on an individual basis. If we are familiar enough with the steps, we will know when they aren't working.

Right now many people have no formula to go by. They don't know where to start. They wind up with a disorganized, lengthy, rambling theses because they lack any format. The one presented here may be an oversimplification, but it works.

Over the years it has been tried on hundreds of people in business seminars. They have returned to say that it has worked in practice. Not just initially, but on an ongoing basis.

Cutting steps to the very basics a large percentage of business memos can be written with the steps shown in Figure 5.5. Just

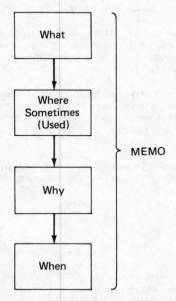

Figure 5.5. Basic Memo Steps.

remembering these three and sometimes four points will at least give us a basic structure.

Let's look at a few examples of memos and real-life business situations and try out the formula. Let's say the roof is leaking in your office and maintenance needs to be contacted regarding getting the situation corrected. First, let's look at a memo that would not be correct; that is, not at all unusual, but not using the steps noted (see Figure 5.6 [Sample 1]). Taking the same example problem, let's write the memo using the four points. This is Figure 5.7 (Sample 2).

Standard Garbled

Memo — Maintenance

(Sample 1)

To: Maintenance	Subject: Leaking roof
From: J. Jones	Date: June 1st.

The roof in my office has started leaking. Each time it rains water starts to drip from several different spots in the ceiling. This is not only doing damage to the ceiling, but is also doing damage to other items in the office.

During last Wedensday's storm, at least three quarts of water leaked in. The books in the mahogany bookcase were damaged, as it was under one of the major areas of concern. The bookcase itself seems to be damaged. Also, one of the file cabinets received water damage to the contents inside. The carpet was also damaged.

I have been searching my files regarding previous memos dealing with this situation. I have not found them yet, but a similar situation occurred about a year ago. I asked at that time that the repairs be made but nothing apparently was done about my request. If someone had repaired the roof then, we wouldn't have the problem now.

It would be appreciated if you would arrange to have the roof fixed as soon as possible. Another rainstorm will cause even more damage.

Sincerely,

J. Jones

Note: "What" and "Why" were answered.
       "Where" and "When" are very vague.

Figure 5.6. Standard Garbled Memo—Maintenance (Sample 1).
(Not Correct)

By going through and answering the four questions the memo falls into correct form. There is no need to ramble on about what is happening. The facts are stated and the request for specific action noted. A date to complete the project is assigned.

It is always important at least to try to establish a firm date. Too often people will give an open-ended time frame such as—"as soon as possible" or "as soon as convenient." This may be a year away to the other party. If you specify a date and they can't meet it, you have the basis to negotiate a date they feel is reasonable. This sets a firm time or target for completion. It also gives you a follow-up schedule.

If the person in question hasn't responded by the date you set, then follow up. Nothing ever seems to get accomplished without a target date. This should be a major goal for each project.

To: Maintenance	Subject: Leaking Roof
From: J. Jones	Date: June 1st.

The roof in my office, located on the 3rd floor — room 11, is leaking. This is causing severe damage to the office furnishings.

It would be appreciated if this were repaired on or before June 5th.

Thank you.

Sincerely,

J. Jones

Note: Brief, courteous and to the point — answers What, Why, Where and When.

Figure 5.7. Maintenance Memo (Sample 2).

Let's follow through and look at another example. This one deals with the internal delivery of the office mail (see Figure 5.8 [Sample 1]). A much simpler format is shown in Figure 5.9 (Sample 2).

This memo adheres to the what, where, why, and when points that were noted. It spells out the customer's needs in a very few sentences. It doesn't go into rumors or possible reasons for the problem, since that is not the function of this manager.

Another example is shown in Figure 5.10. This follows the previous pattern of rambling all over the area. The most important item to be

To: Internal Mailroom   Subject: Mail Delivery

From: R. Brown   Date: July 2nd.

The mailroom has not brought my mail according to schedule for over a month. The 9:00 a.m. delivery and pickup sometimes does not arrive until noon. The 1:00 p.m. until 4:00 or 5:00 p.m. When this happens then the 4:00 p.m. delivery is missed completely, and there are only two mail runs instead of three.

I am not certain what the problem is. Some people have said that the mailroom is short of help. I have heard that several people who have quit have not been replaced. This really is not an excuse, since temporary help can be brought in. This should provide the necessary help until replacements can be found.

If you are looking for people to work in the mailroom, assuming the rumors are correct, you might want to contact Mary Smith in accounting. I understand she has two children just out of high school that may find this position ideal.

I would like to have the mail back on schedule because a large portion of my work in procurement deals with getting invoices out on time. I can only do this if the mail is timely. When the schedules change and I don't get the mail, my invoice scheduling also becomes a problem.

Sincerely,

R. Brown

Note: "What" and "Why" were answered
       "Where" and "When" are very vague.

Figure 5.8. Standard Garbled Memo—Office Mail (Sample 1).
(Not Correct)

considered—"When" is left open. Particularly, in this case, where two months have passed, we need to zero in on the time factor. If not, another two months will pass before anything is accomplished.

The corrected memo in Figure 5.11 (Sample 2) is a little longer than the other corrected samples. The reason for a few added sentences was to nail down this very important time factor. The head of the mailroom who is writing the memo is going out of town. There is no reason the problem has to lie dormant until his return.

Personnel is advised of the what, where, and why of the problem. A definite meeting date has been established to meet the principals and get resolution of the problem. Chances are very good that knowing they will have to respond in the future meeting, personnel will assign the problem an immediate priority.

They would probably like to be able to meet with these managers the next week with the problem solved, or on its way to being solved in the near future. Those problems with the due dates clearly stated

| To: | Internal Mailroom | Subject: | Mail Delivery |
| From: | R. Brown | Date: | July 2nd. |

The mail to my office, second floor room 213, is not arriving on schedule. For the past month deliveries have been late and many even missed. My schedules in procurement are directly affected by these deliveries.

Please return to the original schedule immediately.

Thank you.

Sincerely,

R. Brown

Figure 5.9. Office Mail Memo (Sample 2).

To: Personnel   Subject: Open Positions

From: S. White   Date: July 3rd.

    The mailroom is experiencing problems. Two months ago we lost two of our people. One quit to go to another company for more pay, and another moved out of the state. Since we only have eight people in total, this was a substantial loss to our department.

    When these people left we immediately prepared requisitions requesting replacements and had them approved. They were sent to you immediately. If you check your records, I believe you will find that it was sometime in April, or about two months ago.

    We have only been sent four possible candidates in that time period. Two of these did not want the position because the pay was not sufficient. One decided to take anohter job. The other one had a back problem and said he could not lift the mail bags.

    This has become a problem, since some of our departments are complaining about the mail deliveries. We can't meet our schedules unless we have sufficient staff.

    Your help in sending us qualified applicants would be appreciated.

      Sincerely,

      S. White

Note: "What", "Why", and "Where" answered
      "When" which is very important is left open.

**Figure 5.10. Standard Garbled Memo—Personnel (Sample 1).
(Not Correct)**

tend to get attention; those without tend to drift and sometimes never get resolved.

USING A PROOFREADER

Most good memo writers know the value of having a proofreader. We all have blind spots when reading our own material. We are tied up in the message we want to convey—making certain that we have covered the what, where, why, and when. Our attention becomes focused and little things slip by.

To: Personnel   Subject: Open Positions

From: S. White   Date: July 3rd

Two months ago we submitted requisitions for two replacements in the mail mailroom. We have seen very few candidates, and this is creating severe workload problems.

I would like to meet with the personnel manager and the recruiting coordinator to resolve this problem. Since I will be out of town the remainder of this week, my assistant will call to arrange the meeting for the week of July 27th.

I would appreciate any help you can provide between now and next week.

Sincerely,

S. White

Figure 5.11. Personnel Memo (Sample 2).

These may be little things to us, but they are, or can be major to the person receiving the memo. Figure 5.12 stresses some of these points. Our memo may appear perfect to us, but by accident the name of the receiver may be misspelled or an incorrect nickname used. One item like this and our entire effort may be wasted. We called the person Bob and he only goes by the name Robert. This seemingly insignificant item has probably not only damaged the value of our memo, but impacted negatively on our own image.

How to avoid this? Try to identify people in your organization who can help in proofreading your material before it goes out. It is wise to have every memo screened by at least one person before it is sent. The more important the memo the greater the effort that should be exerted on having it proofread.

Memos going to the president of the company or board of directors should be reviewed by several individuals. Those that are going to have wide distribution, such as to all employees or all department

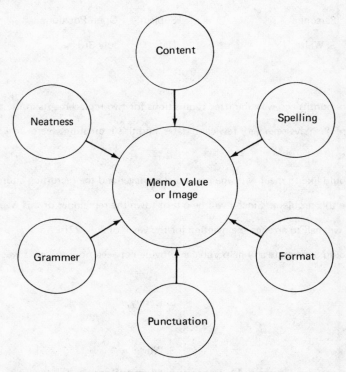

Figure 5.12. Value of Proofreading Memo.

managers should also be proofread by more than one person. The amount of review should be consistent with the amount of possible embarrassment should an error be made. The greater the potential for embarrassment, the larger number of people who should be involved in proofreading it.

6
The Report

What is a report? For our purposes let's try to establish a business definition. A report in business usually details a specific problem, occurrence, or situation. It is usually a study, and in most cases an analysis of the problem, occurrence, or situation.

Reports generally go into depth regarding the topic they cover. They are structured to provide information about their origin as well as factual information that has been researched. They are often used in business as a basis to obtain information to make a decision.

Many people are as afraid of reports as they are of memos. One of the basic reasons is that they don't know how to write them. In fact, they don't even know how to start. This chapter will provide a report format and some sample reports to help eliminate the fear of report writing.

FORMAT

What is a good report format? Let's try to keep this as simple as possible. We could probably dredge up eight or ten different formats, but that would just cloud the issue even more.

Let's use a format that targets on gaining factual data for decision making. Figure 6.1 details such a format. This is close to the standard report format used in most MBA programs.

The first item on the format list is facts. This is the introduction. Here the report writer explains how and why the report is being prepared, and it would be the place to include any prior research or study on the matter at hand. In short, this section brings everyone up to date on how the project got started, and what is known about it.

Next is the discussion/findings section. This is where the study that

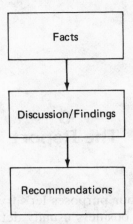

Figure 6.1. A Report Format.

took place is detailed with a description of the various avenues that were explored and what was found or noted in each. Lists of people contacted and their response to questions asked appear in this section. Also included would be the pros and cons of conflicting suggestions or ideas.

This is the area in which to demonstrate the thought process that occurred as the problem or situation was analyzed. It should show that all reasonable avenues were explored.

The last step is the recommendations section. This is where any suggested action would be noted. The findings developed in the prior two sections should make the suggested action obvious. If the facts and discussion/findings sections are developed logically, then the recommendations should develop as a normal conclusion to everything that has gone before.

We can spend an inordinate amount of time talking about a report. For those interested in preparing one the best starting point is to see a couple of actual reports. Figure 6.2 is an actual report.

Following the three simple steps outlined, the report almost completes itself. It takes the guesswork out of what steps to follow. Let's take a look at another example—Figure 6.3.

The full reports are useful to those interested in detail and willing to read the entire package. This probably includes managers with responsibility for implementing the specific actions and selected staff people. Those in the specific departments affected would also want to read the report in detail.

In the case of the report on personnel turnover probably everyone in the personnel department as well as managers plagued by heavy turnover would read it. Those in administration would probably be interested in reading the detail on the word processing study. Those thinking about purchasing or installing a word processing system might also be interested in reading it in its entirety. In order to accommodate the busy executive who would probably be interested in the report content, but not interested in the detail, include an executive summary to make the report 100 percent effective.

EXECUTIVE SUMMARY

An executive summary is a one-page recap of the detailed report. It is a digest summary and usually goes at the very front of the report.

Why does it make the report more effective? It means that your message or findings will be communicated to almost everyone. Even busy executives will normally take time to read one page. Without such a summary, most reports are not read.

Getting your report read, even in summary form, means you have communicated your ideas. Adding an executive summary also means your report is going to be reviewed at the more senior management levels where decisions are made. This is the ultimate goal of any report.

Frequently, the summary generates interest in reading the entire report. The busy executive manager, staff person, etc., may read the summary and say, "Hey, this is valuable information!" and then go on to read the detail.

Without the summary the report may be avoided, or put to one side until time to read is available. This time never seems to come and the report is never read. Without a summary the report's only selling point is the title. If the title isn't specific, again, the report is pushed to one side.

Let's take a look at what an executive summary might look like. In fact, let's take the two reports in Figures 6.2 and 6.3 and prepare executive summaries for them (see Figures 6.4 and 6.5).

Facts:

On August 6, 198—, the Corporate Executive Committee requested a study on the company's employee turnover. Certain members of the committee felt that turnover had recently increased and that could be detremental to further operations.

A special study group was appointed by the Corporate Executive Committee to study the turnover issue. They were asked to see if turnover had increased, and if it had to find out why and to suggest solutions. This group consisted of Mary Smith and Joe Jones of the personnel department, Ken Johnson and Ralph Jackson from Engineering. The group has met every two weeks for the past three months to explore a possible explanation.

Discussion/Findings:

The first step the group took was to review the turnover statistics for the last five years. The turnover statistics from the personnel department's records were as follows:

	Turnover Percentages				
	This Year	Last Year	3 years Ago	4 years Ago	5 years Ago
Managers	10%	5%	4%	3%	3%
Non-Managers	20%	10%	9%	7%	7%

The findings were significant. This years turnover was double for both managers and non-managers when compared with last year. It is approximately three times greater in both cases than four years before.

The study group noted that the turnover situation was critical and steps must be taken to determine what the cause was, and to find possible solutions. The group decided to bring in an outside management consultant who was experienced in dealing with turnover problems.

Three firms were suggested by the Director of Personnel. The group asked for a proposal from each. The XYZ firm was the final choice. The major reason for their selection was the fact that they have previously completed similar studies for four firms in the same industry as ours. This combined with the fact that their price was competitive tipped the scaled in their favor.

Figure 6.2. Personnel Turnover Study.

Personnel Turnover Study
(Continued)

The technique they used to analyze our problem was to sample survey present employees, as well as telephone survey all employees who terminated in the last two years. Their findings were significant. Three of our major competitors accounted for 80% of our turnover — both management and non-management. The basic reason for leaving to join them appears to be a special bonus policy they all implemented three years ago.

This bonus policy offers employees an opportunity to earn an additional 5% to 20% of base salary if they meet selected production goals. The past employees who were interviewed stated this was a significant incentive. The studies indicated that all our other benefit and pay packages were competitive. It also indicated that our past and present employees had positive feelings toward supervisory and management staff.

The XYZ consulting firm has offered to do a cost benefit analysis of our implementing such a bonus system. They indicate that since bonuses are based on meeting increased production goals that the cost to have such a plan may be small. In fact, there is the possibility that with sufficiently increased production that we could actually make money.

In any event, every indication is that by implementing such a system that our turnover would return to normal. The cost savings here will be significant. The XYZ Consulting firm indicates they will include a cost savings study on this as part of their package. The entire cost for the follow on study will be under $5,000.00.

Recommendations:

1. The company should consider going to a bonus program similar to those used by our local competitor. This will, according to our consultants study, stop the excessive turnover.

2. Before implementing such a bonus program, that we commission the XYZ consulting firm to do a cost benefit study. This will provide us with sufficient information to know the cost of our decision.

Facts:

The Director of Administration met with the Operating Committee on September 8, 198—. He pointed out that departments are placing individual orders for word processing equipment throughout the company. This equipment is from different manufacturers and of different capabilities. He questioned whether it wouldn't be advisable to standardize the orders.

The Committee assigned a study group headed by the Director of Administration. Included in this group were Operating Committee Members from manufacturing, engineering, and finance. The following details their study and findings.

Discussion/Findings:

Word processing equipment has become very popular over the past several years. A survey of all departments indicated that there are approximately fifty pieces of word processing equipment scattered around the company. These fifty pieces of equipment are made by eleven different manufacturers.

Under the present system each department is responsible for contacting vendors and ordering their own equipment. If the item is within the department's budget, the department manager may purchase it as he/she sees fit. There is no coordination between departments as to the type of equipment or cost of the items.

An initial cost study shows that the word processors from the eleven different vendors vary in price by as much as thirty seven percent. In no case was volume discount on equipment achieved because none of the purchases were jointly coordinated company wide.

The study group contacted the firm which is doing the data processing study for our new management information system. They assigned one of their experts in the word processing area to advise us. The cost was less than a thousand dollars to review our needs, since they are presently under contract for the major systems study.

Figure 6.3. Word Processing Study.

Word Processing Study
(Continued)

The analyst's study indicated that two of the eleven vendors offered a full range of equipment that would meet our needs in every department. These vendors were then asked for proposals based on being given an exclusive contract. The Y Corporation indicated that they had a backlog of business and could not offer a discount rate of more than 20% for an exclusive contract.

The X Corporation was very interested and offered a 40% discount to act as the exclusive supplier of word processing equipment for the next three years. We would not have to agree to any purchases, but just to use their equipment if we did purchase. Their costs would be fixed at today's rate, so there would be no inflationary creep over the period contracted for.

The proposal was reviewed by the systems analyst and by our legal counsel. Both concurred that everything was in order and that the proposal seemed to be in our best interests at this time.

The study team makes the following recommendations:

Recommendations:

1. That the Director of Administration must approve all purchases of word processing equipment. The budgets for such purchases would be centralized in this area.

2. A contract be signed with the X Corporation as the sole supplier of word processing equipment for our company.

The Corporate Executive Committee noted that turnover appeared high. A special study group from key departments was formed to study the matter.

Statistics showed that manager and non-manager turnover was running three times what it was four years ago. The XYZ consulting group was brought in to study the matter, since they are experienced with turnover problems.

Three of our competitors account for 80% of our turnover. The reason they appear to be attracting our employees is a payment of bonus for performance package which they offer.

The recommendation of the study was to consider going to a similar bonus plan. However, the first step would be a follow on study to determine the cost impact.

Figure 6.4. Executive Summary
Personnel Turnover Study

The Operating Committee was advised that individual departments were placing separate orders for word processing equipment. The Committee formed a study group to look at the possible savings in centralizing these purchases.

The study indicated that the departments are ordering from eleven different vendors, and that prices for similar equipment items vary significantly. A consultant did a brief study and noted two of the eleven vendors offered a complete range of equipment that would meet the needs in every department. One of these vendors offered a 40% discount.

It was recommended that we centralize the purchase of the word processing equipment, and buy from the X Company which offered the large discount.

Figure 6.5. Executive Summary
Word Processing Summary

7
The Speech
and
Audio Visual Aids

There is probably no single experience as frightening in everyday life as getting up before a group to speak. Almost everyone, even professional speakers, have a certain amount of apprehension. If you don't think so, ask a frequent speaker about the way they feel. Most will admit to the same fear we all feel. The professionals have just discovered tricks to mask it.

You may become comfortable with certain speaking experiences. For example, most college instructors feel tense the first time or two with a new class. After that the tension dissipates. However, if the same instructor has to address a faculty luncheon the real fear of being in front of a group returns.

Most outstanding speakers say they are always fearful with a new group. Many professional speakers will admit that they are always ready to run away just before going "on stage." Of course, they don't usually run away, plus they have learned a few tricks so the audience doesn't know how scared they are.

Why are we all scared? We are all scared of making fools of ourselves. In front of a group we are very vulnerable and open to attack. Not only is our personal appearance in the spotlight, but also our gestures, personality, ideas, and so on. At this point in time, a person is truly under the microscope in many ways.

What can we do about the fear? One of the first steps is to recognize that it exists. Don't feel that you are the only one. The only time to be truly concerned is if you aren't fearful and apprehensive.

Next recognize that the duration of absolute terror is going to be relatively short. It usually builds up just before you start to speak and lasts for a minute or two as you get started. However, this short period of time seems like an eternity to all of us.

TRICKS TO DEALING WITH FEAR

There are some things we can do to reduce some of the terror and make sure our audience is not aware of it. First, let's deal with reducing some of the fear itself. Some techniques are shown in Figure 7.1.

When a speaker arrives for a presentation, one of the first things they are usually offered is a cup of coffee. That is probably the last thing they need! Coffee, tea, and many colas contain caffeine and other stimulants. These are just going to add to existing nervousness.

Try to avoid these several hours before a major presentation or speech. If you have an 8:00 A.M. morning speech, and refuse to miss

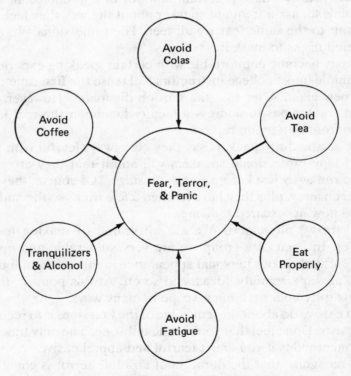

Figure 7.1. Reducing Speaking Fear.

that first eye-opening cup of coffee—try diluting it with water. Everyone's eyes open wide just before getting up to make the speech. Too much coffee may make them pop out.

Many of us, as we get tense, tend to reach for an extra cup of coffee, tea, or cola, etc. It is a nervous reaction that just feeds on itself. If you don't think so try doubling your normal coffee intake and see how jittery you feel.

Eating is another point in question. Some people get nervous and can't eat. No food can mean low blood sugar, and this can result in a certain amount of tension. Each person has to know his or her own needs in this area. If going without food increases tension, try to eat something an hour or so before speaking, even if you don't feel like it. A little soup or peanut butter and crackers can work wonders.

Trying to avoid fatigue before speaking is only common sense. Sometimes, however, it is hard to do this if you are having trouble sleeping several days before a major speech. Again, staying away from stimulants such as coffee and taking moderate exercise can help you relax. Most people have individual techniques for assuring proper rest when under stress. This is a time to employ them.

What about tranquilizers and alcohol? This is an individual matter, but don't rule them out. Of course, you should have your doctor's approval. Many articles and books on speaking automatically say no to their use, and suggest deep breathing exercises or something in their place. But if tranquilizers or alcohol work for you, then use them—but with caution.

Speaking in front of a group is an unnatural state of affairs. Any way you can survive the ordeal should be used. In other words, whatever works for you—use it!

If you are going to use tranquilizers know what their effect is beforehand. Don't take the first one you have ever used just before making the presentation. You might go to sleep just as you are called to the podium!

Try them out during practice sessions and have someone critique your behavior. Know how they affect you and your presentation. Also, remember that the stress in the real presentation is going to exceed that in practice. Even tranquilizers are not going to relieve it all.

The same thing applies to alcohol. At a luncheon or evening meeting, it may be available at the table before speaking. Different people have different levels of tolerance. Some people are more relaxed and speak much better after a few drinks. Others become ill or get "sloshed" and make a fool of themselves. Here again, the time to discover this is not when giving the speech, but beforehand. The real secret is to know what works for you, have your doctor's approval, and test the remedy several times before making presentations.

A double warning. Never mix alcohol and tranquilizers. Also, use them only as directed by your doctor.

PREPARATION

Good preparation is one of the real secrets to making a successful presentation. The stress and jitters will usually go away after the first minute or two if you have prepared. Once into a presentation you know well the tension will start to melt away.

Know your material frontwards and backwards. Practice, practice, and practice, and then practice some more. It is important not only to know the material, but the sequencing and any equipment that you will be using. This is pointed out in Figure 7.2.

One time a person had a well-organized presentation; it was outlined on 3 × 5 cards. He got to the podium and started into the speech. The cards accidentally dropped about a third of a way through. Since they

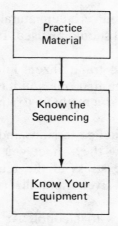

Figure 7.2. Preparation for Speaking.

weren't numbered and he couldn't resequence them rapidly, the presentation turned into a disaster.

Another embarrassing occurrence can take place when someone is using a piece of equipment, say a movie projector. The presentation goes well until the time comes to show the film. But the speaker doesn't know how to use the projector, or hasn't provided for its operation.

Everyone waits while there is a great deal of frantic running about. Sometimes the panic goes on for a few minutes, and sometimes the film never gets started. Regardless of whether the lapse has been for a few minutes or an hour, the presentation has been marred.

All of the items noted are usually avoided by practice sessions. Start such sessions first by yourself. Then invite a few friends or co-workers to view it. Ultimately, it is a good idea to do a trial run with an even larger group.

By this time you should have a good feel for the material, sequencing, and the equipment. Think through some alternatives if something goes wrong; even practice some recovery techniques. Ask those viewing the dry run to challenge you with difficult questions. More often than not the recovery techniques won't be needed, and the questions are seldom as difficult as we fantasize.

USE OF HUMOR

All of us have sat in an audience. We have seen speakers who are terribly nervous, equipment that doesn't work, people confronted with embarrassing questions, etc. We feel terrible usually because we empathize with the speaker. The old adage, "There but for the grace of God go I" holds true.

Audiences want the speaker to succeed; they identify with the person who is speaking. When the speaker is nervous, embarrassed, or hurt so are most of the people in the audience.

If there is an opportunity to inject humor into the presentation, this helps to ease the audience and the speaker's tension; the faster you can do this, the better for everyone. It helps if the first thing a speaker can do is to show a funny slide, tell a joke, etc.

Humor is an area that professional speakers concentrate on heavily; they know it relaxes the audience and entertains as well. It is wise to remember that most audiences aren't usually as interested in the topic as the speaker is. In fact, they may be there only to hear the parts of the presentation that relate directly to their area of concern, interest, and responsibility rather than the whole show. There are others who are there because they are obligated to attend for one reason or another. The more enjoyable you can make the presentation, the better it will be viewed in general.

The humor must fit the audience. We should use the same techniques we would with any other part of the presentation. That is to try it on a small representative audience, or to "dry run it." Those is this test audience can tell you if your humor is on target or not. It is always better to find out with a test, than chance an error.

VISUAL AIDS

One of the advantages of using visual aids is shown in Figure 7.3. The visual aid rather than the speaker becomes the focus of attention. At this point the speaker often becomes "one" with the audience and all the interest, attention, etc., is focused on the visual aid and away from the speaker. This in itself relieves a great deal of tension, both for the speaker and the audience.

Let us next define visual aids. As Figure 7.4 indicates, they are numerous. In fact, this figure contains only a sampling of some of the more common ones. If you were to take a few minutes to think about others, the numbers might even be doubled.

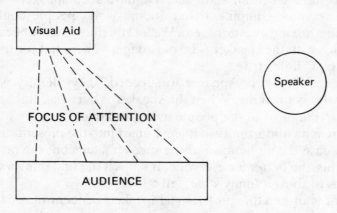

Figure 7.3. Focus of Attention.

Each one has its own characteristics and pluses and minuses. One, the overhead projector, is used so often in the communication aspect of business that we have devoted an entire chapter in this book to it. It is too important a visual aid to be given a brief paragraph or two.

35mm PROJECTOR

This is a very handy audiovisual device used by many speakers. Almost everyone has seen it. It is usually square at the base with a round carousel on top to hold the slides. Most companies have them available for presentations as do most hotels catering to speakers. Figure 7.5 points out the advantages and potential problems.

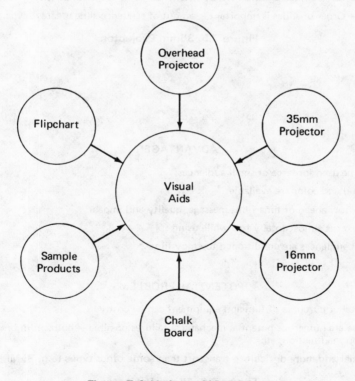

Figure 7.4. Variety of Visual Aids.

ADVANTAGES

- Can be used for large or small groups.
- Compact — easy to carry.
- Slides can be held on screen as long as needed.
- Can reverse to a prior slide.
- Hand held controls for speaker.
- Slides can be in color.

POTENTIAL PROBLEMS

- Slides can be costly — particularly those in color.
- Bulbs can burn out.
- Carousels sometimes have a tendency to jam.
- Control mechanisms held by speaker sometimes malfunction.
- Order of slides is important — an out of sequence slide creates havoc.

Figure 7.5. 35mm Projector.

ADVANTAGES

- Can be used for large or small audiences.
- Sound and color are available.
- We know ahead of time films message, quality and impact.
- Speaker is almost totally free while using.
- Most audiences are conditioned to enjoy films.

POTENTIAL PROBLEMS

- Rental or purchase of film and equipment can be costly.
- There are numerous potential mechanical failures possible — bulbs, film breaking, sound malfunction, etc.
- Bulkier and more difficult to transport than some other types (e.g. 35MM)

Figure 7.6. 16mm Projector.

16mm PROJECTOR

This is the common movie projector. As technology has made its use more simple and compact, we find it has become even more of a tool for use by speakers. An entire business has grown up around providing films and equipment for speakers in almost every category. You can almost name your topic and find a companion film to complement your presentation. Figure 7.6 points out the advantages and potential problems.

CHALK BOARD

Known to everyone and probably considered one of the classical visual aids is the chalkboard. Its use has diminished little over time. Even the advent of technology has not replaced its use, nor made it less valuable. Figure 7.7 points out the advantages and potential problems.

SAMPLE PRODUCTS

Sample or demonstration copies of the products can prove to be a very effective visual aid. This may range from large items such as campers and vans, through vacuum cleaners and mops, to perfumes and marital aids. The old adage that "A picture is worth a thousand

ADVANTAGES

- Inexpensive once in place.
- Little experience or training is needed to use it.

POTENTIAL PROBLEMS

- Cannot be used effectively with large audiences.
- Most are not portable.
- Limited ability to depict real life situations.
- Does not fully draw attention from speaker — nervousness may show up when person tries to write.

Figure 7.7. Chalkboard.

words," is supplemented here by the "Actual item is worth a million words." Figure 7.8 points out the advantages and potential problems.

FLIP CHART

Another classic visual aid that has been around is the old standby referred to as the flipchart. Most briefings and presentations are given with one standing by for possible use. Though not always used even when present, it is well thought of by most in the speaking world. Figure 7.9 points out the advantages and potential problems.

ADVANTAGES

- Understanding is achieved since people view the actual item.
- Questions deal with a real item.

POTENTIAL PROBLEMS

- Large items may create a logistics problem in getting them before the audience.
- Item may not perform as hoped during the demonstration.
- Small items usually limit the size of possible audience.

Figure 7.8. Sample Products.

ADVANTAGES

- Newer models are portable.
- Provides a ready writing surface almost anywhere:
- Pages may be torn off and taped to the wall for the participating group to refer to.
- Few mechanical problems associated with its use.

DISADVANTAGES

- Like a chalk board visual area is limited. Usually best when used with small groups.
- A nervous speaker may have shakey handwriting.
- Ability to write or print legibly is critical.
- Marking pens always seem to run out of ink at the wrong time.

Figure 7.9. Flipchart.

Many beginners feel that they must choose a single visual aid to use during a presentation. This is really not true. In fact, some of the most successful presentations are supported by multiple aids.

As shown in Figure 7.10, a speaker might start out with a 16mm film, use the chalkboard, and ultimately show sample products to his or her audience, interspersing this with a lecture and discussion.

Figure 7.11 shows another sequence of events. Here the speaker starts out using 35mm slides and goes to an overhead projector, again, interspersing the visual aids with the appropriate lecture and discussion to clarify points and answer questions. It should be noted that a flipchart was brought along, but never used.

In the event the discussion had lead to a listing of items, points of interest to be noted, or an item to diagram, the flipchart would have been essential. A good speaker tries to provide for eventualities such as this with backup aids.

There is another factor that should not be overlooked when using multiple visual aids. That is the enjoyment, interest, or entertainment of the audience. Often straight lecture and discussion can be boring. The use of visual aids tends to break the monotony of even a short speech.

This is important with every audience, but particularly important for adult audiences. Business audiences are normally composed of adults who like to be entertained. In fact, they will quickly let their minds drift to other topics if the presentation starts to become boring.

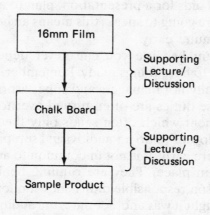

Figure 7.10. Presentation I.

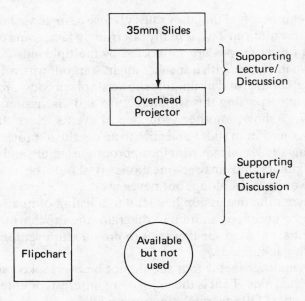

Figure 7.11. Presentation II.

In this case active use of visual aids helps to break up the routine and keep the audience's interest.

EARLY ARRIVAL

When using visual aids for a presentation, plan to arrive early at the place where you are going to speak, this means an hour early, and not just five or ten minutes early.

This is important because you can never depend on hotels or company services to have things ready. Remember, the people doing the setup are usually not managers and supervisors. In fact in large organizations these duties are often turned over to the janitorial or custodial department which often sends only the newest and least experienced employees to do an audiovisual setup.

If you aren't there early, it is not uncommon to arrive and find out no equipment is in place. They are running behind on the setup schedule, the person responsible didn't show up for work, the order was lost, they thought it was another date, the audiovisual equipment

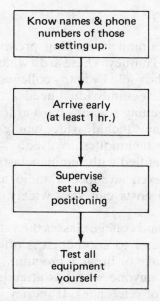

Figure 7.12. Steps in Audio Visual Preparation.

was set up in another room, etc. If you give enough presentations, you will hear all of the excuses.

Nothing is more upsetting than to arrive just before your presentation only to find no audiovisual equipment. This will happen 40 to 50 percent of the time unless you take the initiative to see that it is there.

However, if you arrive an hour or so early you can get the ball rolling and the situation turned around. Have the name and phone numbers of those responsible for setting up your presentation with you. Always order a setup to be ready hours before you start. If questioned, tell them you need to practice.

You will want to be sure that the equipment is functioning properly. Everything should be tested—plugs, bulbs, screens, etc. Try to assure that there will be extra bulbs and someone around for general maintenance if you need them.

Figure 7.12 shows some of the major things we have talked about. Normally, following these steps will prevent a lot of problems. They won't solve every unforeseen event that may arise, but nothing can do this. The best we can hope for is to control events that we are aware of.

FORMAL TRAINING

Many people find training in making presentations an excellent investment in time and money. There are a wide variety of classes and seminars offered on the topic by many colleges and universities, so it is easy to find one to meet individual needs.

Almost all adult evening sessions have at least one, if not several courses available. Many include videotaping and feedback to the students as one of the techniques involved.

The marketplace is filled with seminars lasting one to five days in length. Some of these even have special studios and individual critiques and counseling. The costs can vary widely, so it is wise to shop around.

For most seminars and college classes the value of the program will vary from one instructor to another. It is often the abilities of the instructor that will make or break a program.

If you don't know anyone who has attended a specific seminar before, ask for a list of references. If money is being charged for a course you have the right to know who has attended previously, and how they felt about the class. Students in most evening college classes evaluate the instructors. Ask to see these evaluations.

SPEAKING CLUBS

Many companies have and sponsor speaking clubs. Members critique each other and have contests among themselves or other local clubs. Expert speakers are brought in and they share their knowledge and experience with the group. These usually cost little or the price of a meal, if a dinner or luncheon meeting is involved.

Almost everyone reading this had heard of Toastmasters. It is a group formed to help people in their speaking efforts. There are chapters in most cities, and many people have experienced very positive results from belonging and participating.

INVITATIONS TO SPEAK

One rule of thumb as you progress in your speaking efforts—don't turn down an invitation to speak. The more exposure and opportunity you have, the greater the confidence you will develop in your ability.

When someone calls and asks you to be a speaker, the first reaction is a defensive out. We all have a natural tendency to say *"no!"* For the sake of our growth and development, we have to turn this into a *"yes!"*

PARTS OF A SPEECH

Whether you go through a formal program, join a speaking club, take a class, etc., the parts of a speech will remain the same. They are almost identical to those required in a written presentation (see Figure 7.13). These parts are important to keep in mind, even for experienced speakers.

Each speech must have an introduction or a beginning. It must have a body, or a message—what it is telling the audience. And finally there must be a wrap-up or summary.

This last point may seem to be an insignificant one, but so many people forget about it. Even experienced speakers can become mesmerized by the sound of their own voice and wander on and on. If a format is not established and maintained, communication, which is our target is not achieved.

Humor, if at all appropriate to the speech, should be used frequently and liberally. Most adult audiences want to be entertained. Frequently the difference between a great speech and one that is labeled as good is the amount of humor that is used!

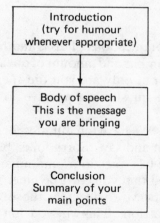

Figure 7.13. Parts of a Speech.

TIME

We are all scared when we get up to give the speech. This lasts a minute or two and usually goes away or is greatly reduced. Once we find that we aren't going to die or freeze up we get on with what we have to say.

As we get into our presentation, we usually start to get a good feeling. We have survived! We have met the challenge! We have conquered! A feeling of elation sets in and we actually start to enjoy ourselves. We are the center of attention—and there is hardly a human being alive that does not love being the center of attention.

This elation causes certain problems. We can lose all track of time. While the first minute or two of fear seemed like hours, hours of elation can seem like a few minutes. Speakers must be aware of this phenomenon.

When practicing a speech, aim at the target time alloted. Remember, nothing will do more to negate all the effort that went into preparing a fine speech than running overtime. During practice emphasize coming as close to the target time as is possible.

There are other methods that may help. Always have the time before you. If a clock isn't visible, place your watch by your notes. Some watches can even be set with an alarm to let you know when you are approaching the last five minutes. Others find that a colleague in the front row can alert them to the passage of time. Just be certain the signals are subtle and don't disrupt the presentation.

QUESTIONS

Do you plan to allow for questions? This is another time consumer. Be ready to control the number and amount of question time. You do this by remembering that not only are you the speaker, but you are the boss. In dealing with questions you have to become an "instant autocrat."

Tell your audience, "We have ten minutes for questions!" and stick to it. You can break in and say, "Sorry folks, but our time is up!" or "we have time for one last question," and mean it.

This is not to suggest that you can't be nice. Tell the audience that the time is up, but that you will meet those who haven't gotten a chance to ask their questions. This way you don't blow the deadline or offend anyone.

8
Using the Overhead

To some it may seem unusual to devote an entire chapter to one type of audiovisual equipment—the overhead. However, if we stop and think about it for a few minutes it probably deserves several chapters, if not an entire book.

The overhead projector is probably the most used and misused piece of audiovisual equipment. Everyone in business has seen one, even if they don't recognize the name. An artist's rendition is shown in Figure 8.1.

It looks almost like a square prehistoric beast. It is boxy in shape with a long arm that comes over the top with a headlike object protruding—an ominous but gentle beast.

It is relatively easy to use; that is easy at least as far as projecting an image on the screen is concerned. There are few moving parts and

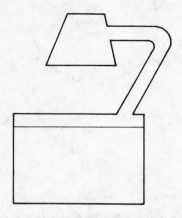

Figure 8.1. The Overhead.

nothing to thread. Turn it on, lay your transparency on the plate, and after some slight focusing, you are ready to go.

Another attractive feature is that an overhead can usually be located without difficulty. They are not terribly expensive, as is the case with movie projectors, so most organizations have a number of them around. They are a permanent fixture in most conference rooms.

Since the cost is not high, there is not a great tendency for them to walk away. This means you can usually locate one without filling out a lot of requisition forms and going to a locked room. Somebody usually has one in the corner of their office or in a cabinet ready to go. It is always pleasant not to have to go on a major treasure hunt to find the piece of equipment for practice or an actual presentation.

The advantages of an overhead projector are shown in Figure 8.2.

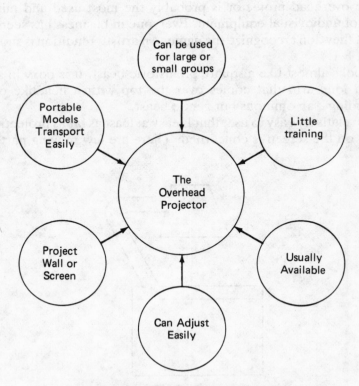

Figure 8.2. Why People Pick the Overhead.

One important feature is that little training is required. Most people following the few simple tips that will be given in this chapter will be able to make successful use of an overhead. Those who combine the tips with a lot of practice will become experts rather quickly.

Overheads are easy to adjust and focus quickly. Nothing frustrates an audience more than waiting while a speaker or his or her assistant spends time trying to get a piece of audiovisual equipment into focus. An overhead generally has only a few simple adjustments. Someone familiar with it can get it into focus in a few seconds.

The ability to project an overhead almost anywhere in a room is a definite advantage. Because you don't require a "silver screen" to be operational you can project against almost any wall or flat surface that is light in color—even shades of beige, light brown, light green, etc., work fine. For this reason many people use an overhead in preference to a screen even when a screen is available.

The portability is another factor. Even the older models, though cumbersome, are fairly easy to move about. You certainly don't have the weight that is normally associated with a movie projector. The newer portable models collapse into a briefcase-size container. These are easy to transport; however, it is wise to practice assembly as some of these can be a bit complex to set up.

Overheads can be used for large or small audiences. The image can be controlled in a small office to a couple of feet in diameter, or expanded in an auditorium to several yards in diameter.

TIPS ON USE

One of the first important tips is to avoid the problem shown in Figure 8.3. Never place yourself between the overhead and whatever surface you are using. This is a very common problem, since speakers seem to be attracted to the spotlight area like moths to a bulb.

If there is a slide on the overhead, the speaker's image blocks it out. If there is no slide, the audience is still distracted by the light shining on the speaker and the speaker's image or shadow on the screen. The basic rule is *always stay away from the front of the projector.*

In the event you are finished showing slides, just turn the machine off. If you are not through, but want to talk for a few minutes, also turn the machine off. This precludes the possibility that you will become mesmerized by the light.

Figure 8.3. Never Stand in Front of an Overhead.

Work From The Side

Figure 8.4 shows where you should be in relation to the overhead. If you are comfortable working to the right of the overhead, position yourself there. If you are comfortable on the left, then position yourself there. The important thing is that you pick a side and stay with it during your entire presentation.

There are some important points to check. First of all be sure that there is room to set your transparencies down. Then be sure that there is enough room for the stack of used transparencies. It is important to keep the two stacks apart to avoid confusion. In other words, you are going to need several feet of working space on the side you have selected.

This may sound like a simple issue that isn't worthy of discussing, but to a speaker it is critical. Often an overhead will be set up by the maintenance crews of a hotel or office and no working space will be

Figure 8.4. Positioning Yourself to One Side.

left. This leaves the speaker two choices—to try juggling all the transparencies in his or her hands or put them on the floor where they usually get stepped on.

Also, when you have chosen a side to work from, make certain other audiovisual equipment is positioned on that side as well. Remember, we want to avoid having to walk in front of the projector light as this distracts the audience.

All flipcharts, chalkboards, etc., should be on the left side if you are working from the left side with the overhead. This, of course, assumes that you plan on using them simultaneously with the use of the overhead. If they will not be used while the overhead is on, then they may be placed anywhere that is convenient.

Avoiding Flicker

Any motion that the speaker makes on the screen plate of the overhead will be magnified on the screen. This is shown in Figure 8.5. For our

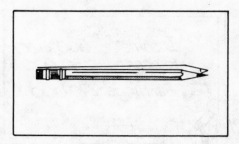

A slight movement of a pencil on the screen plate of the overhead causes a major movement on the projected image.

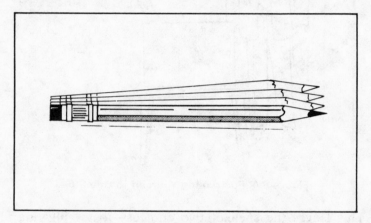

Figure 8.5. Problems of Flicker.

present purposes we will use the term *flicker* to mean any movement on the screen which is not intentional.

We often have to make movements to point out items, outline a sequence of events, etc., but these are not flicker. However, flicker takes place when a pencil unintentionally rolls, as in Figure 8.5, or where thumb or fingers are on the edge of the screen, or an object has inadvertently been placed on the screen.

Another frequent cause of flicker originates in the way a transparency is put on the screen. Many speakers are talking as they put the transparency on, and don't finish placing it. They have it half on the screen and half in hand and are wrapped up in their speech. This is shown in Figure 8.6, and it is a very annoying phenomenon for the audience, since their attention is focused on the screen.

Figure 8.6. A Partially Placed Transparency.

USE OF A PENCIL AS A POINTER

You don't have to go to the projected image when using an overhead to point something out. A pencil can be used effectively as a pointer right on the screen plate of the overhead. Figure 8.7 shows this method.

It is best to lay the pencil on the overhead and slide it forward to the next point you want to make. If your hands are the least bit shaky due to tension this will be magnified when holding either a pencil or a transparency. It is best to put them down on the overhead, and then slide them into the desired position. This keeps the audience from seeing the magnified shaky condition.

A mechanical pencil is usually better than a wooden one, since a

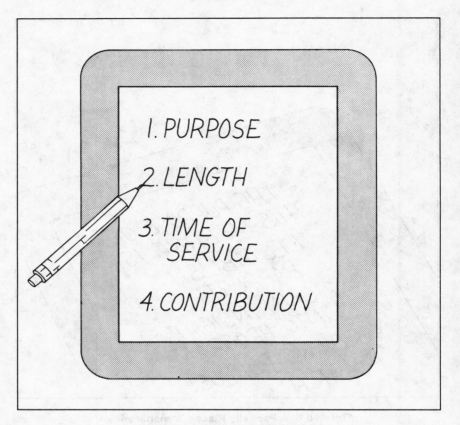

Figure 8.7. Use of a Pencil.

mechanical pencil generally has a pocket clip. The clip keeps the pencil from rolling.

The image of the pencil comes out so clearly on the screen that often the manufacturer can be identified. For this reason some speakers who want to impress their audience will only use a pencil that is known by its distinctive shape to be very expensive. Many people laugh at doing this, but it does give the speaker a certain affluent image. There is a very true old adage that states that "An ounce of image is worth a pound of performance."

Regardless of which pencil you choose as a pointer to reflect your image, make certain you have one before you start your presentation. Too often a speaker will get up, start his or her presentation, then have

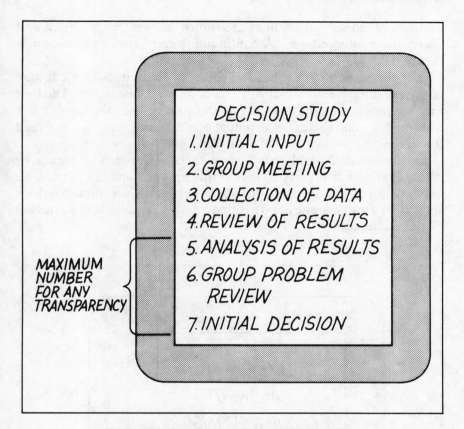

Figure 8.8. Acceptable Lines of Information.

to ask someone in the audience for a pencil to use as a pointer. When speaking, always be prepared even if you have to make up a checklist and go through it like a pilot does before flying an aircraft.

Number of Lines

The number of lines of text that is contained on a transparency is significant. Usually people deal easily with five to seven lines of information. This is pointed out in Figure 8.8.

Now, let's say we have twelve lines of data that relate to the same study that was done in the last figure. The way to handle this is to show them on two separate transparencies. In this situation you might want to divide them so that six lines are shown on one transparency, and six on the continued one. A continuation transparency is shown in Figure 8.9.

In some cases you may have to show an entire document. It may consist of multiple lines that will exceed the rule just stated. The best way to handle this may be to put the title of the document on a transparency and to distribute actual copies to the audience and read it together.

Another related problem is when we show a detailed schematic or diagram. There is no way to divide this up into separate parts. The only thing you can do is to distribute copies as just mentioned, or show it on a transparency and assume a certain amount will be missed by the audience.

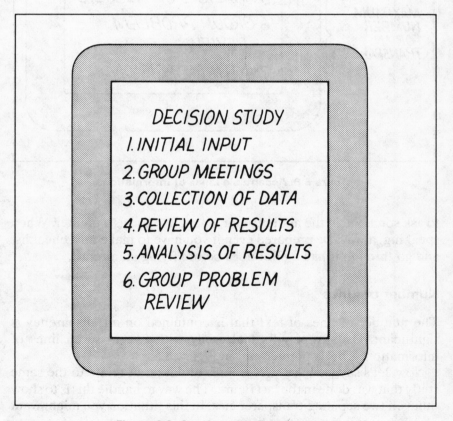

DECISION STUDY
1. INITIAL INPUT
2. GROUP MEETINGS
3. COLLECTION OF DATA
4. REVIEW OF RESULTS
5. ANALYSIS OF RESULTS
6. GROUP PROBLEM REVIEW

Figure 8.9. Continuation Transparency.

Preparation of Transparencies

We have been talking about how to use transparencies. A topic that may be just as important is how to prepare the slides themselves. There are certain tricks in this process that will make your presentation more effective.

One thing is the choice of color: Slides come in a wide range—clear, yellow, blue, red, green, etc. The most commonly used is clear. The only problem is that this color tends to give off more of a glare than the others. Many professionals will use a soft yellow that does not create a glare. It is also wise to interject a red or green transparency to emphasize a point.

For example, you might have the introduction in green, the main

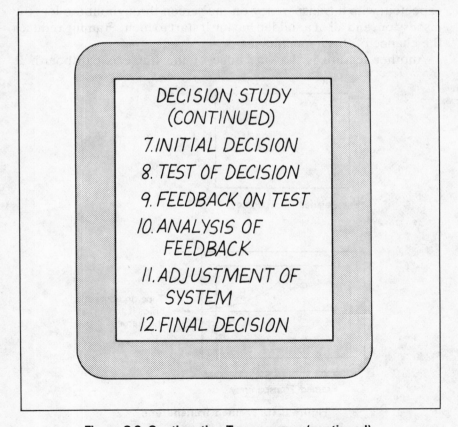

Figure 8.9. Continuation Transparency (continued).

body of the presentation in yellow, and the conclusion in red. These are choices best left to the individual presenter's creativity.

Another item is the use of cardboard frames. These are usually available in any stationery store where the transparencies themselves are sold. The transparency is affixed to the frame with scotch tape. The transparency with and without frames are shown in Figure 8.10.

There are a number of advantages to having the transparencies framed rather than loose. First, when they are not framed there is a tendency for them to stick together which makes them hard to handle during a presentation.

Also, an unframed transparency is a thin piece of plastic-type material. If it is left too long on the heated face of the overhead projector it will start to melt. Nothing is more embarrassing than to be in the middle of a talk or discussion that has gone on longer than expected, with a transparency on the screen throughout the lengthy discussion, and all of a sudden having it start to melt. Framing reduces the chance of this happening.

Another feature is that the edge of the frame is cardboard. It

Regular Transparency

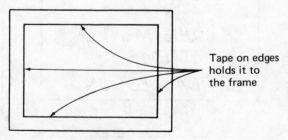

Tape on edges
holds it to
the frame

Framed Transparency

Figure 8.10. Framed Transparency.

provides a place to number the slides and even write reminder notes. These can be very handy when giving a presentation. The slides stay in order and you may not even need notes other than the ones on the frames.

Writing on the Transparencies

In some instances special marking pens are used to write on the transparencies while talking. Some instructors use this technique in the classroom in place of writing on a chalkboard. One of the problems is that this technique creates flicker that was discussed earlier. It is very annoying to an audience.

Professional speakers usually have their slides typed in large block letters, or hand lettered by a professional. It is wise to have all transparencies prepared ahead of time, and avoid any writing on them during the presentation. This creates the professional image all presenters seek.

9
Communicating
With
Subordinates

A manager's job is to get things done through the medium of people. If you look around there are very few good managers. Most managers don't realize that their task is to guide and direct others; most are involved in doing the work themselves.

Even at the executive levels too often we find "working managers." They are preparing proposals, writing contracts, etc., in fact doing everything but managing. Why are they doing this? The answer is probably because most don't realize what being a manager really means. They can't let go of the past projects they were involved in before being promoted. Also, they are not able to derive satisfaction from getting things done through others.

This probably compounds the communication problem. Since most managers aren't performing their own function, they often miss out completely on providing guidance to subordinates. We can't fully address this problem here, but we can provide some guidelines that will aid good, and not so good managers in communicating with their subordinates.

WHY SOME SUPERVISORS FAIL

Too often communication with subordinates is a limited one-way process, as shown in the upper half of Figure 9.1. The supervisor is telling the subordinate what he or she wants done in one case. In the other case the subordinate is feeding limited information to the supervisor on what is happening. But in return the supervisor gives nothing to the subordinate but instructions.

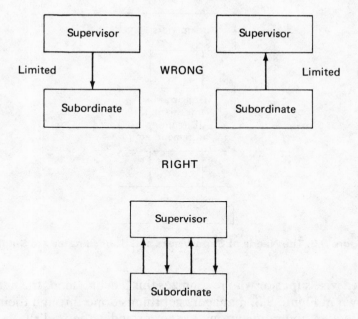

Figure 9.1. Communication With Subordinates.

Some people may feel this is the way things should be done. Particularly autocratic supervisors may see nothing wrong in this arrangement. However, they themselves do not want to be treated by their bosses in this manner. They want what almost all of us want, an exchange of information.

Those involved in management surveys find that the chronic complaint at all levels is about poor communication. People feel they are not being kept informed. Superiors consistently feel they have a need for more information from their own superiors, but often fail to recognize the same needs in the people who report to them.

This is depicted in Figure 9.2. People at all levels must have information about the functioning of the organization. What is our organization's goal or goals? How is the organization doing? What are my goals and how are they measured? This list could go on forever.

People, be they managers, executives, laborers, etc., all want to know what is going on. This is why grapevines and other informal communication systems spring up. People have a need for information and they are going to get it one way or another.

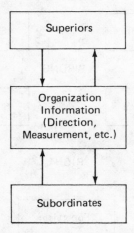

Figure 9.2. The Needs of Supervisors and Subordinates are Similar.

It is a wise superior who recognizes this fact and feeds the need. As is shown in Figure 9.3, managers get things done through their staff. An effective communications system provides the fuel that assures that the actions the staff takes are the desired ones. The better informed the staff members are the better their performance will be.

IMPROVING STAFF COMMUNICATIONS

How does a superior go about setting up communications systems that work? One of the first things any supervisor can do, as noted in an earlier chapter, is to hold regular, frequent staff meetings at the same time every week.

Many supervisors shy away from staff meetings fearing they will have to spend hours in preparation. If they do spend a lot of time on preparation they are holding the wrong kind of staff meetings. As was noted in an earlier chapter, the meeting should consist of those people who report to a specific superior. This usually keeps the staff meeting small and manageable, and most important of all, everyone present participates in the discussion. The heart of the meeting is each person's contribution of what is occurring in his or her work area.

In addition, meetings may be held in order to make special announcements. These are sometimes purely informational and may

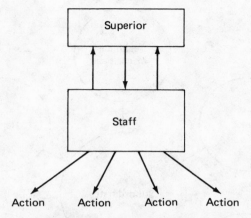

Figure 9.3. Staff is the Action Agent.

not consist of an exchange of information other than a few questions. The groups may be larger than just a few people. These types of meetings are held usually to make announcements such as a contract award, plant move, etc.

The secret for success of such meetings is timeliness. They must be held when the information is first received. If they are held later, the information will already be out through informal channels (the grapevine). It is better to hold no meeting at all than to hold a meeting where the information is stale or yesterday's news.

Another useful means of maintaining good communication is for a supervisor to circulate printed material that comes across his or her desk. Figure 9.4 depicts some of the types of material to which each supervisor has access.

This is an area of communication many supervisors overlook. They are often on distribution lists that their people are not on, and the act of sharing these documents opens up a whole new area of communication between superior and subordinates.

For example, many supervisors receive technical magazines. Sharing them with subordinates is appreciated. The supervisor may attach a note suggesting an applicable article, and this also means a lot because it helps everyone stay current in their field.

Supervisors may receive letters, memos, or reports that subordinates may not normally be on distribution to receive. If these are not totally confidential they should be forwarded to subordinates. They can only

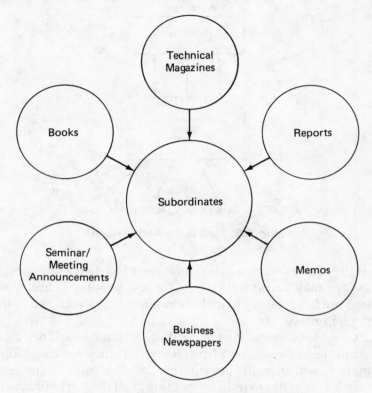

Figure 9.4. Circulation of Printed Material.

improve everyone's knowledge base of what is going on in the organization. In the long run this type of interchange of materials improves the effectiveness of the organization.

Business newspapers as well as seminar/meeting announcements are routinely read and discarded. Would such information be of interest to your people? If so, it only takes a few minutes to route them and may pay dividends in improving subordinates' knowledge of what is happening in their field.

Books may be harder to route because of the length of time needed to read them. However, a particular book may be of specific value to a specific subordinate. Should the book be of significant interest or use maybe the unit budget can stand the cost of several copies. A library

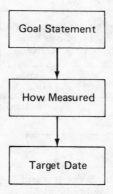

Figure 9.5. Components of Goal Setting.

of technical books for your area can pay dividends to everyone in a department.

Another way a supervisor can open up channels of communication is by meeting individually with those reporting to him or her. One of the major things most subordinates want to know is what is expected of them and how are they doing. This actually makes the supervisor's job easier.

Figure 9.5 provides a good format to follow. Figure 9.6 shows the process to follow in order to achieve this aim.

The first step is for the supervisor to request that the subordinate prepare a list of his or her goals, including the target dates involved. Usually, the goals should be about six or eight in number. This is a commonly used management technique often called "management by objectives."

These goals must include significant projects. They are not just a repeat of the individual's job description, but items the person can control. Often these are goals that cannot be accomplished unless special attention is focused on them.

Once the subordinate has completed the list of goals, these are submitted to the supervisor for review. He or she then can agree or disagree with the goals, as might be appropriate. In some cases there may be a duplication, since another employee is working on a particular goal. In other instances the supervisor may want to add a goal or change a target date based on department goals.

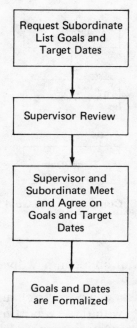

Figure 9.6. Steps in Goal Setting.

The supervisor and subordinate should then meet and go over the list. There should be agreement that the goals are reasonable as well as the target dates. Both should agree on how completion of the goals will be measured.

The agreed-to list actually serves a couple of purposes. One is the obvious benefit of identifying goals, target dates, and measurements. It acts as a catalyst to help the organization get necessary work identified, structured, and accomplished.

The other thing that it does is to set the stage for communication between superior and subordinate. Figure 9.7 indicates normal future steps. We don't want to just establish goals and then review them at the end of the year. The real benefit is the communication which occurs in a periodic review and discussion. This should occur at least quarterly if not even more frequently.

Situations in an organization change and the goals must also be

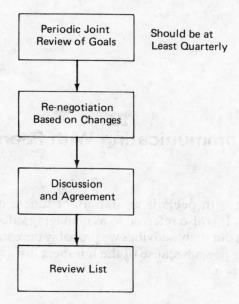

Figure 9.7. Goal Follow-Up.

flexible. This periodic review allows for a renegotiation based on this changing environment. Goals need to be modified, and at the same time target dates adjusted. This gives everyone a chance to discuss what is happening in the organization, and what direction it is taking. This is a major communication benefit for everyone involved.

10
Communicating With Peers

Communicating with peers is an important function that all of us have to perform. It is also referred to as managing sideways, as shown in Figure 10.1. In our daily activities we probably have more continuous contact with our peers because of the numbers involved, than we do with our supervisor.

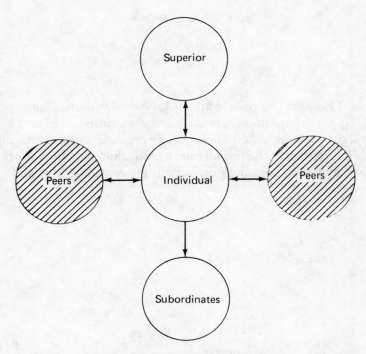

Figure 10.1. Managing Sideways.

Our peers are by definition those people who are at the same level in an organization. However, in most organizations this distinction is often blurred. For our purposes we should be looking at peer groupings. The people whom we consider peers may be those in staff positions that we consider to be on an equal level with our own. It may also contain people in other departments who are at a higher or lower level, but do not have direct authority over us, or vice versa.

In business, working relationships tend to define peer groups rather than a strict level in the organization. This is shown in Figure 10.2. The group shown encompasses some people at the same level, some at a little higher level, some at a little lower level, and a staff position.

COMMUNICATION BETWEEN GROUPS

Communication between peer groups is usually more open at the lower levels of an organization. This is shown in Figure 10.3. At the upper end of the organization structure politics comes into play.

This is not to say that politics is not spread throughout the

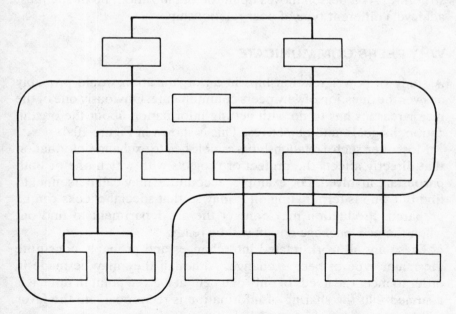

Figure 10.2. Peer Groupings. In business, working relationships tend to define peer groups rather than a strict level in the organization.

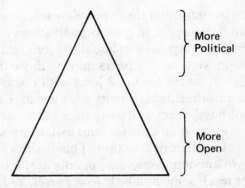

Figure 10.3. Variation by Level.

organization. It is intense at the upper echelons because the rewards are greater, fewer slots are open for promotion, and because of the psychological makeup of people who achieve these positions. These are the areas, as the saying goes where they play hardball. An individual can improve his or her peer communication by recognizing this structure. As a person moves up in the organization, he or she must achieve a different type of peer relationship.

WHY PEERS COMMUNICATE

A study of power relationships in an organization would probably answer the question of why peers communicate. Obviously one of the major reasons has to do with getting information about the organization, its goals, and objectives. This is shown in Figure 10.4.

Most often such a relationship is established to exchange information that directly affects the project or projects with which one or both parties are involved. For example, accounting may call personnel to find out who is terminating on Friday so that special checks can be prepared. Production may contact the art department to find out when the new package design will be ready.

These are all work related interchanges and probably constitute the major type of peer exchange. Although they may be made in order to meet the needs of only one peer at a given point in time, it is assumed that the sharing of information is reciprocal and the favor will be returned in the future.

Figure 10.4. Reasons for Peer Communication.

A certain amount of exchange is to be chalked up to comradery or pleasure—the people are communicating because they are on friendly terms. People on the same approximate level deal with similar problems, concerns, people, situations, etc., and they often enjoy sharing their experiences with each other.

OPPORTUNITIES FOR CONTACT

The makeup of one's peer group can vary based on organizational structure. For example, if you work in a large centralized accounting group your contacts are more frequently those in the accounting department.

Now, let's assume the accounting department is decentralized. Two- or three-person groups of accountants are assigned to line organizations to service them. In this case a different set of peer relationships will develop. They will be based more on the line of people the accountants have daily contact with rather than those in the traditional accounting department. This is shown in Figure 10.5.

Centralized Accounting

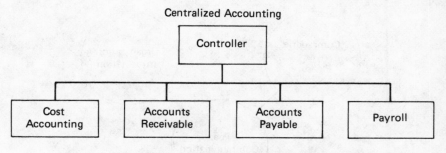

In a centralized function peer groups tend to be parochial.

Decentralized Accounting

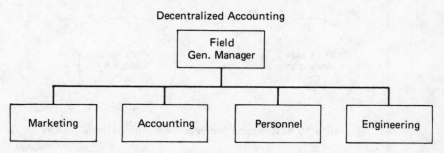

Figure 10.5. Centralized versus Decentralized.

CHEMISTRY IN PEER GROUPS

An important factor in the formation of any group is that magic ingredient called "chemistry." It is the establishing of instant liking or a psychological fit. It is something we all feel when it exists, but really never know what to do about when it is missing.

Peer relationships where strong positive chemistry exists will be strong; where the chemistry is weak, so will the relationships be weak. And where the chemistry is at odds, there will often be open hostility.

CORPORATE POLITICS

Corporate or organizational politics will impact on peer relationships; for example, if the accounting department head is feuding with the head of marketing. This type of conflict is apt to impact on all levels in the department.

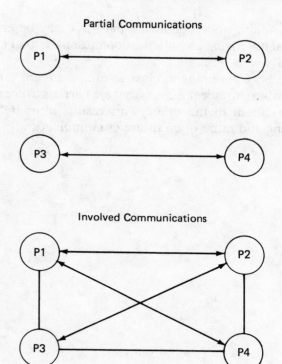

Figure 10.6. Peer Communication.

IMPROVING PEER RELATIONSHIPS

Good relations with peers is an important ingredient for any organization. Peer communications as shown in Figure 10.6 demonstrates the people both partially and totally involved in communicating with one another.

Obviously every supervisor, manager, etc., wants to create an environment with totally effective communication. This, of course, accepts the premise that total communication is a valid aim. It takes a strong manager to accept this because a certain amount of control is lost in the process. We then enter into the realm of allowing participation in management.

One technique to achieve this is through team-building exercises. These can be conducted by third-party experts knowledgable in the techniques. Again, since organizational lines may be crossed, such approaches at improving communication must have total management support at all levels.

There are books, seminars, classes, etc., on team building. The basic premise is to surface the issues that are barriers to communication and confront them in the open. This results ultimately in a new understanding and more open future communication.

11
Communicating With Superiors

Communicating with superiors is also referred to as managing upwards, as is shown in Figure 11.1. Everyone wants to communicate well with their boss. Each of us finds that this is easier with some bosses than others.

Different personality types and different styles of management can make communication easy or almost impossible. If it is easy, life can seem very pleasant. When it is hard, it can be the exact opposite.

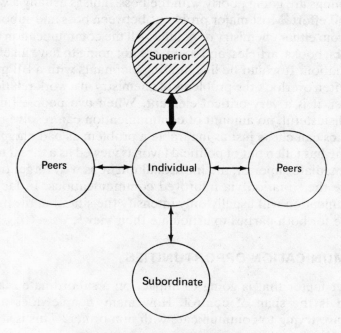

Figure 11.1. Managing Upward.

This chapter has little to say to those who find communicating with their supervisor very easy. A few things that may further improve this situation may be identified. However, it is doubtful that we want to touch this situation. If it is good, let's leave well enough alone.

By the same token, it is doubtful that this chapter is going to do much to help the person who is "at war" with his or her supervisor. Improving communication is not going to turn this situation around, and anyone believing that is just kidding themselves. The person involved is going to have to transfer out of that supervisor's jurisdiction, or leave the organization.

CHAPTER'S USE

Figure 11.2 gives some idea of the areas where the material in this chapter may help in improving upward communication. Basically, it is going to help when "average communication" with the supervisor is occurring.

People tend to turn their efforts toward improving communication when things are going poorly with the boss. This is usually a waste of time and effort. Most major problems between boss and subordinate result from either chemistry or politics. All the communication classes, seminars, books, articles, and so on, are not going to have an effect on this situation. It would be like hunting elephants with a BB gun.

We often overlook the problems of chemistry in a work relationship. However, it is a very critical element. When two people find each other distasteful, no amount of communication can resolve this.

Politics can cause just as incurable a problem as bad chemistry. If someone has fallen out of political favor, is viewed as a threat to his or her immediate superior, the individual might as well forget trying to improve the situation via improved communications. In fact, good communication will usually only intensify the situation by making it possible for both parties to articulate their views.

COMMUNICATION OPPORTUNITIES

Another factor that is going to impact on a subordinate managing upward is the span of control. How many people does a supervisor have trying to communicate with him or her? This is shown in Figure 11.3.

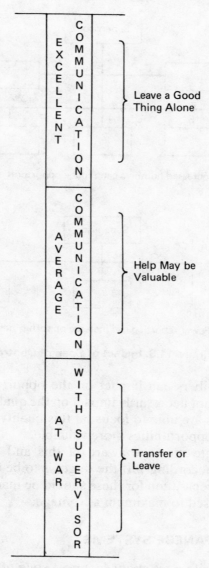

Figure 11.2. Improving Upward Communication.

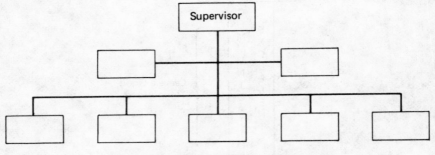

Increased numbers can reduce opportunities.

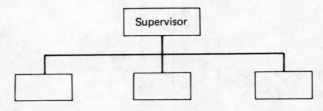

Fewer reporting can increase opportunities.

Figure 11.3. Impact of Span of Control.

The sheer numbers can impact on the opportunity for contact. However, it does not necessarily impact on the quality of the contact. Some supervisors are able to focus on this quality aspect and make shorter meeting opportunities more valuable.

The subordinate must be aware of this and gauge his or her communication accordingly. If the target is to be a few high-quality meetings, then preparation for these should be made accordingly, so that the time is used to maximum advantage.

IMPACT OF JAPANESE SYSTEMS

Today we hear quite a bit about Japanese style of management and communication. As Japan has become a leader in the production of a wide range of commodities, attention has focused on their management techniques and communication systems. The problem is that too many firms merely identify what is being done in a given situation, and

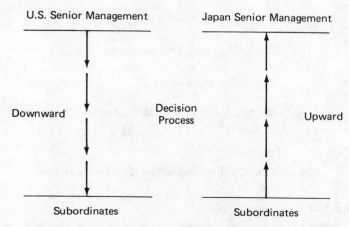

Figure 11.4. U.S. and Japanese Communication Contrasts.

try to emulate it across the board, without first being sure that a particular system is really right for their needs.

This attitude has caused, and probably will continue to cause, a large number of problems for both management and employees— supervisors and subordinates. One of the big factors in superior/ subordinate relationships that has been overlooked is that there are significant philosophical and cultural differences between Japan and other nations.

Figure 11.4 points out one significant difference in the communications area. In the United States decisions are made at the upper level of management and filtered downward. In Japan it is the reverse. Input from lower levels moves upward, consensus is attained, and top management acts as the final arbiter. This is somewhat of an over-simplification, but should suffice for our purposes.

Communication with superiors differs significantly between these two countries and two cultures. This does not mean that there is not something we can learn from the Japanese about communication. It does, however, mean that we can't automatically overlay one of their systems onto one of ours without a great deal of analysis. The cultural differences may be so significant that a particular system may not only be unworkable, but a disaster. This is shown in Figure 11.5.

IF

Culture I ≠ * Culture 2

Then Very Likely

Communications I ≠ * Communications 2

* ≠ Does not equal.

Figure 11.5. Cultural Impact on Communications.

SEVEN STEPS

There are certain things that someone with average communications abilities can do to be more successful in interacting with his or her supervisor. In fact, following these steps can take someone who is of average ability as a communicator to a position where their abilities are outstanding. These steps are shown in Figure 11.6.

1. First identify the boss's goals and objectives. You need this information in order to be able to deal constructively with your supervisor. People's behavior and interests can generally be predicted if you know what their goals are.

2. Find out what portion of these goals and objectives is yours to accomplish. A supervisor uses subordinates to accomplish his or her own goals, and each one has a portion of them to perform. If you don't know what your portion of the target is—ask!

You can't accomplish anything if you don't know what is expected. You can waste a lot of time and do damage if you are working on the wrong problem. Also, find out what the timetables are. When are you expected to have your portion of the goals completed? This can also be a critical issue. Being late with a goal does not improve your standing.

3. You must know what you can do to make your supervisor look good while completing the goals. This may involve telling others of the value of the goals, how they contribute to the organization, how they improve morale, etc. Anything you can do to make your supervisor look good will make you look good, and improve the communication channels between you.

4. Be open about showing effort toward the goals. Communicate

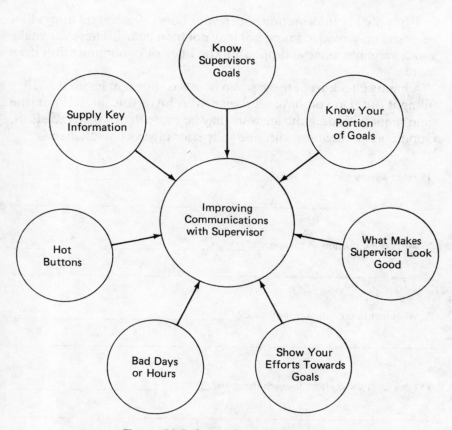

Figure 11.6. Seven Steps to Success.

by regular status reports, either oral or written. Keep your supervisor appraised of your efforts before being asked. Be proactive rather than reactive!

5. Recognize that everyone has bad days or hours. Trying to establish communication during these times can be difficult and even risky. If Monday or late afternoons are times when your boss is usually not in a good mood, try to avoid meetings then at all costs. Try to schedule at other times when you know communications will be better. Make the odds in your favor.

6. Know your boss's "hot buttons"; that is, what makes him or her angry. Everyone has them and a wise subordinate finds them out and uses them to his or her communication advantage.

7. Supply key information. Keep your boss informed on things that he or she may need to know, but may not have heard. These can make you a valuable asset and open up the lines of communication even more.

A handy checklist of these seven points is shown in Figure 11.7. Try filling it out. Do you have all the answers? Are you sure? If not, the time spent in finding the answers may be more than worth the effort. Good communication with one's superior always pay dividends.

1. What are my superior's goals? _____

_____

2. What is my portion of these goals? _____

_____

3. What makes my superior look good? _____

_____

4. How can I show effort towards the goals? _____

_____

5. What are the boss's good/bad days or hours? _____

_____

6. What are my superior's "Hot buttons"? _____

_____

7. How can I better supply key information? _____

_____

Figure 11.7. Checklist for Supervisor Communication.

12
Conclusion

In chapter 1 we explored the question of definition. It was determined that the intent of this book was to focus on the business aspects of communication. It was decided that the target was to provide a number of practical techniques and concepts to help the individual in business in his or her speaking and writing on the job.

It was pointed out that the end product of speaking and writing in a business environment is to accomplish tasks. The aim being to get things done with the least amount of effort and then to move on to the next task.

The impact of communications on various levels was reviewed. One of the significant items pointed out was the importance of the hidden organization shown in Figure 12.1. Formal structure does not control communications to the degree some believe. In fact, in many organizations the informal or hidden organization may dominate the communications channels.

Chapter 2 dealt with the staff meetings. These were defined as a regular meeting between supervisors and subordinates. The importance of these meetings was heavily stressed.

It was suggested that staff meetings should be held regularly, usually weekly, and at the same time and day of the week. A separate conference room with a circular table or seating arrangement was recommended.

Staff meetings are probably the most important meeting held in most organizations. This is pointed out in Figure 12.2. Staff meetings contribute three important activities in any business: communication, problem solving, and education.

Too many supervisors avoid staff meetings because they fear having to do a lot of preparation. A really good staff meeting should not

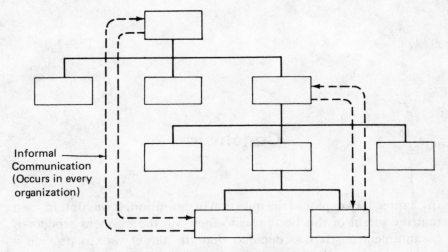

Figure 12.1. Hidden Organization.

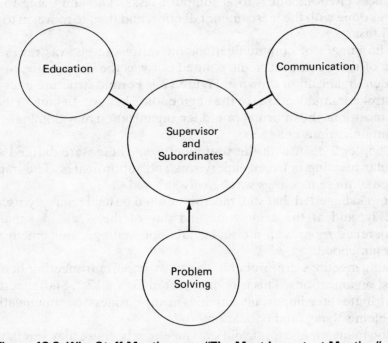

Figure 12.2. Why Staff Meetings are "The Most Important Meeting".

require large amounts of preparation. The key to this is having a roundtable or round robin discussion where each member shares what is going on in his or her area.

This is a critical point in conducting truly effective staff meetings. It also serves to take the pressure of conducting the meeting off the supervisor. In addition, it gives the members a feeling of ownership because they are active participants.

Chapter 3 dealt with large group meetings. There seemed to be universal agreement that small groups were in the range of seven to ten people or less. This was based on the closely paralleled management concepts of "span of control" and what constitutes an "effective" and "productive" group. Obviously, for our definition large groups are those that exceed these guidelines.

Even though people joke about large groups, often referred to as committees, they continue to exist. If they weren't performing some function of value, businesses would have done away with them a long time ago.

Figure 12.3 probably holds the key to the existence of large groups. They are very effective in performing the functions of education and communication. Problem solving, though, seems most effective when handled by small groups.

Chapter 4 dealt with individual meetings. It pointed out that very few people are truly effective in business unless they have developed the ability successfully to conduct meetings with individuals. We

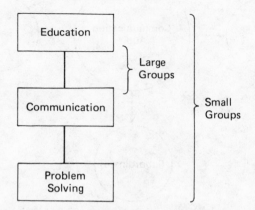

Figure 12.3. Functions a Group May Perform.

know there is a correlation between success and the ability to communicate on an individual basis.

It was recommended that most people in business might benefit from an individual communications audit. Figure 12.4 shows what this might entail. It would be a survey of how one communicates with superiors, subordinates, and peers. Feedback such as this can be invaluable for anyone's career.

The importance of planning and being prepared for individual meetings was stressed. Some of the techniques for relieving individual meeting tension were discussed. The importance of the business luncheon, and how to use it effectively was reviewed. It was noted that real communication is going to exist at the end of the lunch when people are most often relaxed, comfortable, and ready to listen with interest.

Tactics for dealing with the emotional individual were discussed. All of us have to deal, at one time or another, with people who are

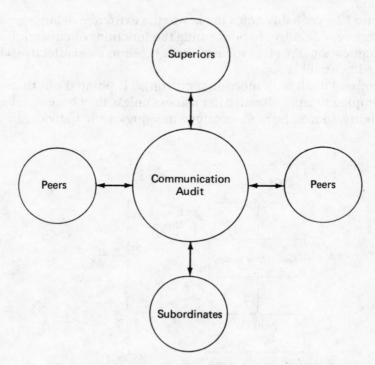

Figure 12.4. Focus of Individual Communications Audit.

crying or angry. There are certain techniques that can ease this situation and open up communication channels. These were explored.

Chapter 5 reviewed the importance of the memo in business, and pointed out some techniques in using memos more effectively. Many people hate to write memos, yet find they must do so to survive in the business world. People usually hate writing memos because they make the task too difficult for themselves and don't employ some organizational tricks.

When people employ the basic memo steps shown in Figure 12.5 the task becomes easier. Memo haters frequently become memo lovers, or at least better memo writers. The chapter then goes on to show various ways to improve memo writing.

Chapter 6 describes the report, which in similar fashion to the memo, is often looked on as an unpleasant chore. Again the solution seems to be in following a comfortable format. Figure 12.6 shows such a format.

The chapter points out the importance of a one-page executive summary. It assures that the report will get more attention by making a quick review easy for the busy executive. Samples of reports and executive summaries are provided for those interested in having a pattern to follow.

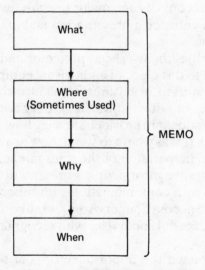

Figure 12.5. Basic Memo Steps.

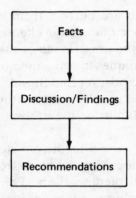

Figure 12.6. A Report Format.

Chapter 7 deals with making a speech and the use of audiovisual aids. It points out that even experienced speakers are nervous and tense. A variety of techniques to deal with anxiety are reviewed. This includes a whole list of things from avoiding caffeine, through possible use of tranquilizers, to proper preparation and practice. The tension will never go away completely, but we can learn to control it and use it to advantage.

Visual aids were discussed in some detail. Figure 12.7 lists the major ones. The pros and cons of each major one are reviewed. Visual aids properly used can enhance a presentation and make a good speaker an outstanding one.

Chapter 8 describes the overhead projector and its use. An entire chapter is devoted to this piece of audiovisual equipment because it is the one most often used in business. It is also the one most often misused by people who don't know the proper techniques.

A series of illustrations are provided showing how to use an overhead. These include such tips as where to stand, how to avoid flicker, using a pencil as a pointer, preparation of the transparencies, etc. Following these steps can improve most people's presentations.

Chapter 9 deals with communication with subordinates. As Figure 12.8 points out, the needs of supervisors and subordinates are similar. It is a wise and successful supervisor who recognizes this and tries to meet these needs.

The chapter stressed the importance of goal setting. It not only assures that necessary tasks are achieved, but is one of the major ways

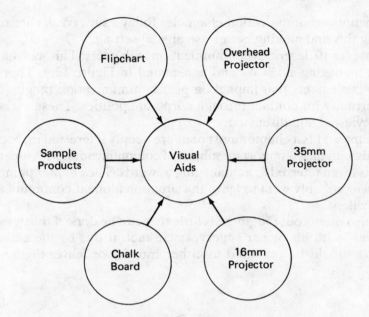

Figure 12.7. Variety of Visual Aids.

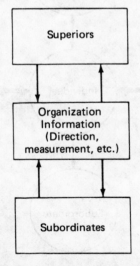

Figure 12.8. Needs of Superiors and Subordinates are Similar.

to open up communication channels. Today's supervisors are recognizing this and making better use of goal setting.

Chapter 10 describes communication with peers. This was referred to as managing sideways and is depicted in Figure 12.9. There are various elements that impact on peer communication ranging from opportunity for contact through corporate politics. These variances are reviewed and discussed.

Chapter 11 is a chapter most of us are deeply interested in, because it deals with the all-important subject of communication with superiors. This is often referred to as managing upwards. The chapter points out that we probably want to leave the situation alone if communication is excellent.

It also points out that there is little that can be done if the person is "at war" with his or her supervisor. In fact, if this be the case, the person should be prepared to either transfer or leave. Figure 12.0

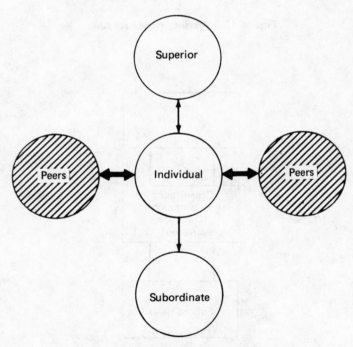

Figure 12.9. Managing Sideways.

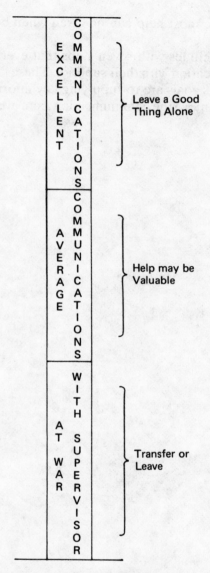

Figure 12.10. Improving Upward Communication.

points out that the most help can be given when communication is "average."

Chapter 11 concludes with seven steps that everyone can take to improve communication with their superior. These range from finding out what the boss's goals are to supplying key information. Working on these seven can move the communication from average to excellent.

Index

Index

proofreader, 48
proofreading, 49
psychological bond, 15

Questions, 74

Rambling thesis, 43
relieving tension, 33
report format, 52, 116
reports, 51-58
roundtable, 13, 113
roundtable discussion, 14-15

Sample agenda, 12
sample memos, 45-49
sample products, 67-68
sample reports, 55-58
seminar/meeting announcement, 92
seminars, 72
shared pressure, 14
show and tell, 14
single visual aid, 69
skilled management, 27
sloshed, 60
small group, 8, 19, 21, 23, 113
span of control, 18-19, 104-105, 113
speaking clubs, 72
speaking world, 68
staff communications, 90
staff meeting, 8-9, 13, 16, 20, 90, 111-112
staff meetings, 111
stand-up meeting, 9
steps to success, 109
stimulants, 60-61
stress, 61-62

subcommittee, 21, 24
success, 114
supportive feeling, 15

Target audience, 23
target date, 45, 93
tea, 60-61
team building, 9, 101-102
technical books, 92
tension, 59, 63-64
third party experts, 101
time, 74
Toastmasters, 72
tongue tied, 27
training and development, 29-30
transpariences, 78, 83-86
tranquilizers, 60-62, 116
tricks, 59
treasure hunt, 96
two way communication, 26

Unforseen event, 71
universal agreement, 18
upper echelons, 98
upward communications, 105-119

Value judgement, 16
visual aids, 64-65, 116-117

War with supervisor
wide distribution, 49
work info, 99
work related problem, 36
working relationships, 24-25, 97
written records, 41